The MAILBOX

Fascinating Facts
SOCIAL STUDIES
100 Comprehension-Building Activities

- **Explorers and Explorations**
- **Revolutionary War**
- **Westward Movement**
- **U.S. Constitution**
- **U.S. Government**
- **Citizenship and National Symbols**
- **Historic Figures**
- **U.S. Regions**

Also includes a ready-to-use review game!

Managing Editor: Debra Liverman

Editorial Team: Becky S. Andrews, Kimberley Bruck, Diane Badden, Thad H. McLaurin, Marsha Erskine, Peggy Hambright, Amy Payne, Karen A. Brudnak, Juli Docimo Blair, Hope Rodgers, Dorothy C. McKinney, Juli Engel, Joanne Mattern, Jennifer Otter, Christine Thuman, Patricia Twohey

Production Team: Lori Z. Henry, Pam Crane, Rebecca Saunders, Chris Curry, Sarah Foreman, Theresa Lewis Goode, Greg D. Rieves, Eliseo De Jesus Santos II, Barry Slate, Donna K. Teal, Zane Williard, Tazmen Carlisle, Kathy Coop, Marsha Heim, Lynette Dickerson, Mark Rainey, Amy Kirtley-Hill

www.themailbox.com

©2007 The Mailbox®
All rights reserved.
ISBN10 #1-56234-753-5 • ISBN13 #978-156234-753-6

Except as provided for herein, no part of this publication may be reproduced or transmitted in any form or by any means, electronic or mechanical, including photocopying, recording, or storing in any information storage and retrieval system or electronic online bulletin board, without prior written permission from The Education Center, Inc. Permission is given to the original purchaser to reproduce patterns and reproducibles for individual classroom use only and not for resale or distribution. Reproduction for an entire school or school system is prohibited. Please direct written inquiries to The Education Center, Inc., P.O. Box 9753, Greensboro, NC 27429-0753. The Education Center®, The Mailbox®, the mailbox/post/grass logo, and The Mailbox Book Company® are registered trademarks of The Education Center, Inc. All other brand or product names are trademarks or registered trademarks of their respective companies.

Manufactured in the United States
10 9 8 7 6 5 4 3 2 1

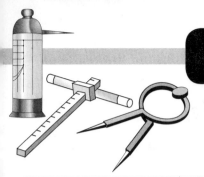

Table of Contents

What's Inside

100 Reproducible Activities

Inside this book, you'll find activities that support 50 essential social studies topics. Each topic is reinforced with two engaging reproducible activities that can be used together or separately.

Featured Topic

Fascinating Fact

Brief Reading Passage

A second fun activity further reinforces the skill.

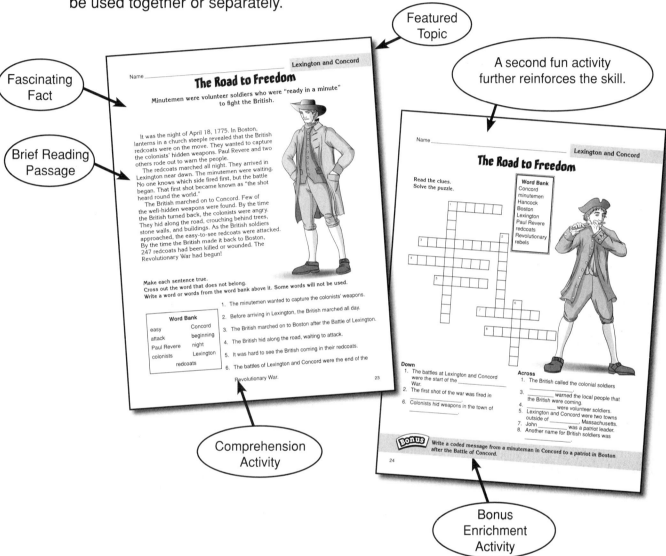

Comprehension Activity

Bonus Enrichment Activity

Ready-to-Use Trivia Game

On pages 105–120, you'll find an exciting trivia game containing 150 cards that review all 50 topics covered in this book. Use the game to review just one topic or use all the cards as a fun year-end review. The game cards also make great flash cards for review.

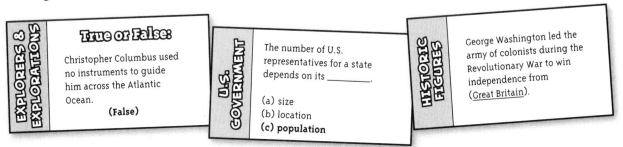

Use Fascinating Facts: Social Studies as

- morning work
- a center activity
- homework
- enrichment
- remediation
- work for early finishers
- small-group practice
- independent practice

Use Fascinating Facts: Social Studies to

- engage students in the learning of social studies
- integrate reading with social studies
- provide independent practice of key social studies concepts
- strengthen comprehension of nonfiction texts
- provide extra practice for struggling readers
- introduce a new social studies topic
- review content before a test
- provide practice with answering questions in different formats

SAILING FOR SPICES

Christopher Columbus and his ships landed on a Caribbean island.

In 1492, Christopher Columbus and about 90 men left Spain on three ships. Columbus thought that he could find a sea route to Asia. Europeans wanted the gold and spices that were there. He guided the ships across the vast Atlantic Ocean. He used only a compass, a half-hour glass, and his instincts. The ships reached a Caribbean island about ten weeks later. Columbus thought he had found the East Indies and searched for gold and spices. He didn't find the spices. He only found small amounts of gold.

Columbus returned to Spain with just a few gold trinkets and some native people. He still convinced the Spanish to send him on three more voyages. He never found a sea route to Asia. But his journeys exposed people on two continents to each other and to new plants, animals, and diseases. The world was changed forever.

Answer the questions.

1. Why did Columbus want to find a sea route to Asia? _____

_____

2. How long did it take Columbus to reach land? _____

3. How many times did Columbus try to find a sea route to Asia? _____

4. What were the lasting results of Columbus's voyages? _____

_____

Name _____

SAILING FOR SPICES

Use the code below to complete each fact.

1. Christopher Columbus was born in ___ ___ ___ ___ ___ , ___ ___ ___ ___ ___ .
   7 5 11 12 1   8 16 1 9 19

2. In 1453, the ___ ___ ___ ___ ___ ___ ___   ___ ___ ___ ___ ___ ___ controlled the
   12 16 16 12 10 1 11   5 10 13 8 14 5

   eastern land route to Asia.

3. King ___ ___ ___ ___ ___ ___ ___ ___ ___ and Queen ___ ___ ___ ___ ___ ___ ___ ___
   6 5 14 4 8 11 1 11 4   8 15 1 2 5 9 9 1

   gave Columbus support for his voyage.

4. Columbus miscalculated the earth's ___ ___ ___ ___ ___ ___ ___ ___ ___ ___ ___ ___ ___ .
   3 8 14 3 17 10 6 5 14 5 11 3 5

   This is one reason Columbus landed in the Caribbean instead of Asia.

5. Two of Columbus's ships were ___ ___ ___ ___ ___ ___ ___ ___ . These were sturdy
   3 1 14 1 18 5 9 15

   wooden ships that could sail against the wind.

6. At one point there was almost a ___ ___ ___ ___ ___ ___ .
   10 17 16 8 11 19

   Columbus's sailors were nervous because they'd been at

   sea a month without reaching land.

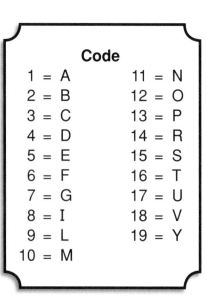

Code

1 = A	11 = N
2 = B	12 = O
3 = C	13 = P
4 = D	14 = R
5 = E	15 = S
6 = F	16 = T
7 = G	17 = U
8 = I	18 = V
9 = L	19 = Y
10 = M	

7. The first islanders Columbus met were ___ ___ ___ ___ ___ .
   16 1 8 11 12

   They farmed, made their own cotton cloth, lived in villages,

   and had social and government systems.

Bonus Columbus didn't find a sea route to Asia on his first voyage. On the back of this page, write a paragraph that he could use to convince the Spanish king and queen to allow him to search again.

©The Mailbox® • Fascinating Facts: Social Studies • TEC61067 • Key p. 121

Exploring for Spain

Ponce de León was one of the first Europeans to claim part of North America for Spain.

Juan Ponce de León was a Spanish explorer. Some even think that he traveled with Christopher Columbus on Columbus's second voyage to America. Others think that he first came to the island of Hispaniola in 1502. Ponce de León led Spanish forces against the native people there.

In 1508, Ponce de León left to explore the island of Puerto Rico. He took over the island and became its governor. He forced the native people to mine gold. Later, King Ferdinand sent him to explore north of Cuba. Ponce de León landed on Florida's northeast coast on April 2, 1513. He thought it was an island and named it "La Florida." He was one of the first Europeans to claim part of America for Spain.

In 1521, Ponce de León returned to Florida to start a colony. He was attacked by native people and wounded by an arrow. He and his men fled for Cuba, where Ponce de León died.

Draw a line to match each sentence starter with the rest of its sentence.

1. Ponce de León wanted to start a colony in   Florida.

2. Some think Ponce de León sailed with   arrow.

3. Ponce de León was governor of   north of Cuba.

4. King Ferdinand sent him to explore   the island of Puerto Rico.

5. Ponce de León died from a wound caused by an   Columbus.

Juan Ponce de León

Exploring for Spain

Read the clues.
Solve the puzzle.

Word Bank

colonize	mine	Puerto	Spain	Ferdinand
claimed	Hispaniola	voyage	Fountain	attacked

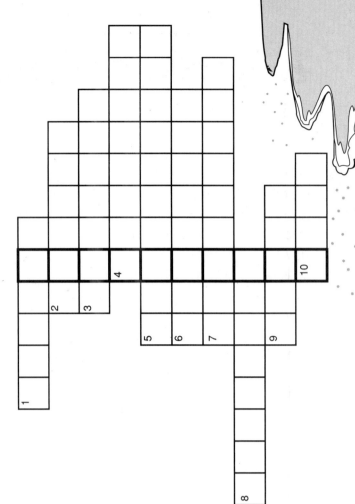

1. Ponce de León may have sailed with Christopher Columbus on Columbus's second _____ to America.
2. He conquered _____ Rico and became its governor.
3. Ponce de León _____ Florida for Spain.
4. Legend says that Ponce de León searched for the _____ of Youth.
5. Ponce de León first settled on _____.
6. Ponce de León was killed when he was _____ by native people.
7. King _____ ruled Spain during Ponce de León's time.
8. Ponce de León tried to _____ Florida.
9. Ponce de León was born in _____.
10. He forced the native people of Puerto Rico to _____ gold.

Write the letters from the bold boxes, in order, to complete the sentence below.

While sailing near Florida, Ponce de León discovered the _ _ _ _ _ _ _ _ _.

Bonus
Legend claims that Ponce de León was searching for the Fountain of Youth. What would the world be like if such a fountain existed? Explain your thoughts in a paragraph on the back of this page.

©The Mailbox® • *Fascinating Facts: Social Studies* • TEC61067 • Key p. 121

Name_____   Francisco Coronado

A Quest for Gold
Coronado passed over treasure without knowing it!

Francisco Coronado explored the southwestern United States in search of the Seven Cities of Cibola. These cities were said to have gold and other treasures. He and a group of more than 1,300 people left Mexico and headed north. They marched for nearly five months. They crossed rugged peaks and arid deserts. They suffered from snakebites, hunger, and Indian attacks. Finally, Coronado's group reached the first "golden" city in New Mexico. They fought to take over the crowded village and then found no gold.

Then Coronado heard about a golden city in the east. He marched to another village in what is now Kansas. Again he found no gold.

Coronado and his men returned home believing that they failed. Years later silver, copper, and other valuables were found in the American Southwest. The metals were below the ground that Coronado and his men traveled over.

Complete each sentence. Use the passage.

1. Coronado and over _____ people set out to find the Seven Cities of Gold.

2. The cities were _____ of Mexico.

3. The first "city of gold" was in _____ _____.

4. No _____ was ever found by Coronado or his men.

5. Silver, copper, and other metals were later found underground in the American

_____.

©The Mailbox® • Fascinating Facts: Social Studies • TEC61067 • Key p. 121   9

A Quest for Gold

Read the statements.
Underline each cause in green and each effect in yellow.

1. The Spanish had heard tales of golden cities, so they wanted to explore the American Southwest.

2. Coronado was determined to find the Seven Cities of Cibola because he believed they held great wealth.

3. A priest was chosen to go on the journey since he claimed to have seen one of the golden cities.

4. When they reached the city and found no gold, the men became discouraged.

5. Coronado and his men became excited when they heard about another golden city in the east.

6. Because they wanted to find the gold, the men marched all the way to Kansas.

7. They were disappointed again since the stories weren't true.

8. Because Coronado found no gold or riches, his trip was seen as a failure.

Bonus

Many other Spaniards explored the area that is now the United States, including Hernando de Soto, Pánfilo de Narváez, and Lucas Vásquez de Ayllón. Find out what each explorer was looking for and the part of the United States he visited.

Exploring the Mississippi

France once owned part of the United States.

It's true that France once owned part of the United States, thanks to French explorer Robert La Salle! La Salle settled in Canada in 1666. He led the first European group that traveled the length of the Mississippi River. He hoped to control fur trading in the areas around the river.

In 1682, La Salle began his trip in present-day Illinois. About eight weeks later, he reached the Gulf of Mexico. He placed a cross and a stone marker near the mouth of the Mississippi. Then La Salle claimed the land around the river and its tributaries for France. He had no idea that the region stretched from the Appalachians to the Rockies. He named the area Louisiana in honor of King Louis XIV of France.

Make each sentence true by crossing out the word that doesn't belong. Write a word from the word bank above it.

1. La Salle explored the Ohio River.

2. La Salle hoped to gain more wealth by continuing to trade land.

3. His journey down the Mississippi River ended at the Gulf of California.

4. He claimed the lands around the river and its tributaries for Spain.

Word Bank			
furs	France	Mississippi	Mexico

12 Name _____

Exploring the Mississippi

Robert La Salle's Travels, 1679–1682

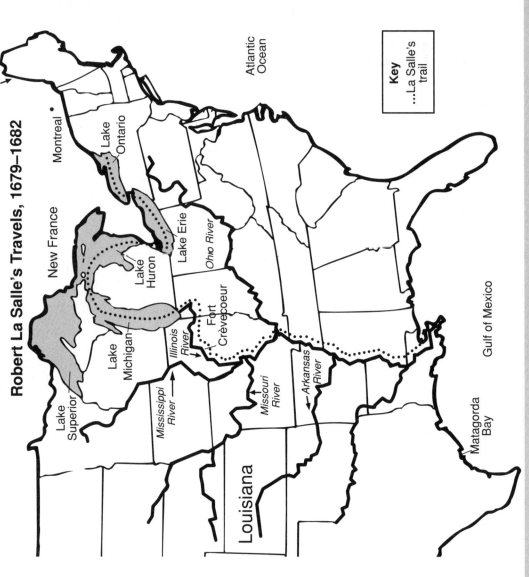

Montreal •

St. Lawrence River

New France

Lake Ontario

Lake Huron

Lake Erie

Ohio River

Lake Michigan

Lake Superior

Illinois River

Fort Crèvecoeur

Mississippi River

Missouri River

Arkansas River

Louisiana

Matagorda Bay

Gulf of Mexico

Atlantic Ocean

Key
....La Salle's trail

Write "true" or "false" next to each statement.
Use the map to help you.

_____ 1. Montreal is east of the Mississippi River.

_____ 2. The St. Lawrence River is east of the Great Lakes.

_____ 3. Fort Crèvecoeur lies along the Missouri River.

_____ 4. The Great Lakes flow into a river that empties into the Pacific Ocean.

_____ 5. The mouth of the Mississippi River is in Canada.

_____ 6. The Mississippi River empties into the Gulf of Mexico.

_____ 7. The Illinois, Arkansas, Ohio, and Missouri Rivers are all tributaries of the Mississippi River.

_____ 8. La Salle's journey ended at Fort Crèvecoeur.

_____ 9. La Salle claimed all of the land south of New France for the French.

_____ 10. Matagorda Bay lies east of the Mississippi River.

Bonus

La Salle claimed the Louisiana region for France. The region stretched from the Appalachian Mountains to the Rocky Mountains and from the Great Lakes to the Gulf of Mexico. Which modern-day states are in this region?

©The Mailbox® • Fascinating Facts: Social Studies • TEC61067 • Key p. 121

FATHER OF NEW FRANCE

Champlain was one of the first to suggest constructing a canal across Panama.

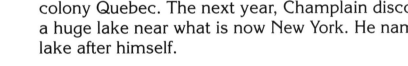

Samuel de Champlain was a French explorer. He is often called the Father of New France. New France was French-claimed land in Canada. He also made several trips to the West Indies, Mexico, and Panama.

After returning to France, he wrote a book about his trips. He wrote about how much he liked Mexico City. He even suggested constructing a canal across Panama. This book was interesting to King Henry IV. The king asked Champlain to sail to Canada to explore the St. Lawrence River in 1603. He was looking for a route to Asia.

Champlain never found this Northwest Passage. However, Champlain returned to Canada in 1608 to start a fur-trading post. He found a spot along the St. Lawrence River. He built a fort there and named this new colony Quebec. The next year, Champlain discovered a huge lake near what is now New York. He named the lake after himself.

Circle the letter of the best answer.

1. Samuel de Champlain explored for _____.
   a. Spain   b. England   c. France

2. He started a settlement in _____.
   a. New France   b. South America   c. Florida

3. He went to Canada searching for a route to _____ .
   a. Asia   b. India   c. Mexico

4. Champlain named a _____ after himself.
   a. city   b. lake   c. river

FATHER OF NEW FRANCE

Unscramble the letters to reveal the place.
Then write a sentence that tells what you learned on page 13 about this place.

1.
`__ __ .   __ __ __ __ __ __ __`
T S   A C E E L N R W

_____

2.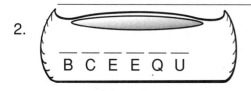
`__ __ __ __ __ __`
B C E E Q U

_____

3.
`__ __ __ __   __ __ __ __ __ __ __ __`
E L K A   A A C I H L M N P

_____

4.
`__ __ __ __   __ __ __ __ __ __ __`
L E K A   I O T N O R A

_____

5.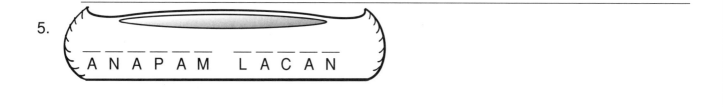
`__ __ __ __ __ __   __ __ __ __ __`
A N A P A M   L A C A N

_____

 **Why do you think Samuel de Champlain is called the Father of New France?**

Search for the Northwest Passage

Henry Hudson was set adrift in a boat and never heard from again.

Henry Hudson was an English sea captain. Little is known about his early life. An English firm hired him in both 1607 and 1608. They wanted him to find a northern sea route to Asia. On these trips, Hudson sailed farther north than any other explorer before him. Both times ice blocked his path, so he returned to England.

In 1609, Hudson sailed for the Dutch. He discovered the Hudson River in present-day New York. The English funded Hudson's final journey in 1610. He discovered the Hudson Strait and Hudson Bay. Hudson thought he'd found the Pacific Ocean. His boat became stranded by ice. After surviving a harsh winter, his crew became angry. They put Hudson, his son, and a few loyal crew members in a boat. The crew set the boat adrift in James Bay. Hudson, his son, and the crew members were never heard from again.

Write "true" or "false."

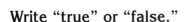

_____ 1. Henry Hudson sailed for the Dutch and the English.

_____ 2. Much is known about Hudson's childhood.

_____ 3. Hudson ended his first two voyages because his path was blocked by Native Americans.

_____ 4. He discovered a river, a strait, and a bay.

_____ 5. Hudson had a very loyal crew on his last journey.

Search for the Northwest Passage

Write a word from the word bank to complete each sentence.

Word Bank

sundial	sandglass	quadrant	pincer
nocturnal	cross-staff	compass	astrolabe

1.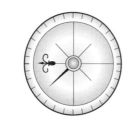
A _____ was used to tell directions (north, east, south, and west).

2.
An _____ gave the location of a ship by measuring the positions of the sun and stars.

3.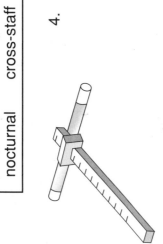
A _____ - _____ was used to sight the stars and find a ship's position.

4.
A _____ helped sailors determine altitude.

5.
A _____ told the hour of the day.

6.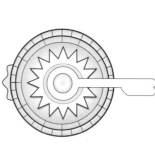
A _____ told the hour of the night by using the stars.

7.
A _____ measured time in hours or half hours.

8.
A _____ was used to mark off each day's progress on a map.

BONUS

Henry Hudson was set adrift in a boat in James Bay. If you were Hudson, which of the instruments above would you most want to have? Explain your answer on the back of this page.

©The Mailbox® • *Fascinating Facts: Social Studies* • TEC61067 • Key p. 121

Colonizing Virginia

John Smith's leadership made Jamestown a successful colony.

John Smith was an English soldier. In 1607, he landed in Virginia with 104 other settlers. They were sent to find gold and start a new colony. Smith was tough and smart. He soon realized that searching for gold in Virginia was a waste of time. The colonists needed to find food and make a Jamestown fort that was safe. But many colonists refused to work.

During the first year, many people died from disease, starvation, and Native American attacks. Then Smith became the colony's leader. He told the colonists they could not eat unless they worked. With Smith in charge, the colony did well. The people traded with the Native Americans for food. There were also fewer conflicts with the local tribes. The tribes were afraid of Smith. In 1609, Smith was wounded by a gunpowder blast. He had to return to England. After he left, the colony was almost wiped out.

Draw a line to match each starter with the rest of its sentence.

1. With John Smith's leadership,   or go without food.

2. The colonists were sent to Virginia   he was wounded.

3. Smith told the colonists to work   were afraid of Smith.

4. Smith left Jamestown after   the Jamestown colony did well.

5. The local Native Americans   to find gold and start a new colony.

Colonizing Virginia

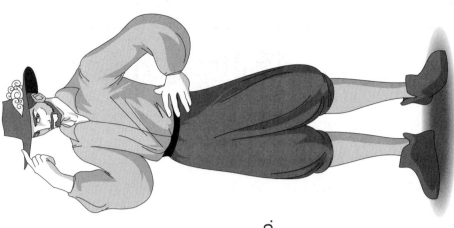

Match each cause to its effect.

Causes

_____ 1. An English company placed ads for settlers to colonize Virginia. They promised "fields of gold and jewels."

_____ 2. Virginia's summer was much hotter than England's.

_____ 3. No one planted crops during the summer of 1607.

_____ 4. Smith was elected president of the colony.

_____ 5. Smith treated the Native Americans harshly.

_____ 6. In September 1609, Smith was injured and returned to England.

Effects

A. By December 1607, the food was almost gone.

B. He made a rule that colonists had to work if they wanted to eat.

C. The heat and humidity sapped the settlers' strength.

D. The colony missed Smith's leadership.

E. The Native Americans began to hate the colonists.

F. Many men volunteered hoping for quick wealth.

Bonus   Imagine that you are John Smith. List five rules you would enforce to help the colony become more successful.

©The Mailbox® • *Fascinating Facts: Social Studies* • TEC61067 • Key p. 121

No Right to Tax

American colonists were not welcome in the British Parliament.

England wanted money from the colonies. They needed to pay for the British soldiers serving in America. So the British Parliament passed a new law in 1765 called the Stamp Act. It said that stamps must be purchased for all important papers in America. Legal papers, newspapers, and even playing cards needed stamps.

The colonists got angry! They did not think they should have to pay this tax. Colonists were not allowed to serve in the British Parliament. The slogan "no taxation without representation" became the colonists' protest.

A group called the Sons of Liberty was formed. Its members fought against the Stamp Act. Sometimes they burned the stamps and bullied the British stamp agents. A few agents were tarred and feathered! Many agents quit. It was hard to sell the stamps in America. So the British gave up on the Stamp Act and cancelled it in 1766.

Complete each sentence. Use the passage.

1. The Stamp Act of 1765 was supposed to raise money for British _____ in America.

2. The Stamp Act said that each _____ _____ had to have a special stamp.

3. The colonists did not want to pay a tax without _____ in Parliament.

4. The _____ _____ _____ fought against the Stamp Act.

5. The British Parliament revoked the Stamp Act in the year _____.

20 Name _____

No Right to Tax

Complete each sentence.
Use the word bank.

To Our American Colonists:
  We need money to pay the British _____
in America. These soldiers protect you. So we have
passed a new law. We call it the _____.
_____. You will need a special
_____ for each important
_____. You will have to pay for
_____ each stamp.

            Sincerely,
            King George and the
            British _____

Word Bank

Stamp Act   Parliament

paper   soldiers   stamp

To King George and the British Parliament:
  We are _____! Why should we pay taxes?
We _____ are not allowed to serve in Parliament.
Making us pay _____ without a say is not right!
The Sons of Liberty will scare your tax _____,
and they will not be able to sell the stamps.

            Sincerely,
            The _____ Colonists

Word Bank

collectors   taxes

angry   American   Colonists

BONUS If you lived at the time of the Stamp Act, would you have supported the king or the colonists? Explain.

©The Mailbox® • *Fascinating Facts: Social Studies* • TEC61067 • Key p. 122

One Boston Night

The participants of the Boston Tea Party swore one another to secrecy.

In 1773, the British government created the Tea Act to help a struggling British tea business. The law said that this tea company could sell its tea in the colonies for a low price. This law would hurt the colonial merchants because a tax still had to be paid on the tea they sold. The colonists thought that if they agreed to pay this tax, they would be taxed even more. When three ships arrived in Boston, the colonists wouldn't let the tea on land. One night, a group of colonists in disguises boarded the ships. They threw 342 chests of tea into the harbor. This later became known as the Boston Tea Party.

Today, we still don't know all the names of the people who dumped the tea that night. The group members swore one another to secrecy. Partial lists of names do exist. And only one man, Francis Akeley, went to prison for this event.

Write "true" or "false."

_____ 1. The British government wanted the colonists to pay a tax on tea sold by colonial merchants.

_____ 2. The colonists were happy to pay the tax.

_____ 3. Three ships tried to bring tea to the colonies.

_____ 4. Colonists threw 142 tea chests into Boston Harbor.

_____ 5. All of the participants of the Boston Tea Party went to prison.

Name _____

One Boston Night

Cut out each box.
Glue them in the correct order in the comic strip below.

1.

2.

3.

4.

5.

6. *Intolerable Acts*

BONUS On the back of this page, draw and explain the next picture that might appear in this cartoon if it continued.

©The Mailbox® • *Fascinating Facts: Social Studies* • TEC61067 • Key p. 122

"Psst. The king has gone too far this time!" "Boston Harbor will be a teapot tonight!"

"I'll show the colonists who's boss! Now they'll have even more rules to follow."

"What do you mean the king says I still have to pay taxes on tea sold by colonial merchants?"

"You must obey the king's orders. You must obey the Tea Act!"

"Send those ships back to England!"

December 16, 1773—The Boston Tea Party

Name _____

The Road to Freedom

Minutemen were volunteer soldiers who were "ready in a minute" to fight the British.

It was the night of April 18, 1775. In Boston, lanterns in a church steeple revealed that the British redcoats were on the move. They wanted to capture the colonists' hidden weapons. Paul Revere and two others rode out to warn the people.

The redcoats marched all night. They arrived in Lexington near dawn. The minutemen were waiting. No one knows which side fired first, but the battle began. That first shot became known as "the shot heard round the world."

The British marched on to Concord. Few of the well-hidden weapons were found. By the time the British turned back, the colonists were angry. They hid along the road, crouching behind trees, stone walls, and buildings. As the British soldiers approached, the easy-to-see redcoats were attacked. By the time the British made it back to Boston, 247 redcoats had been killed or wounded. The Revolutionary War had begun!

Make each sentence true.
Cross out the word that does not belong.
Write a word or words from the word bank above it. Some words will not be used.

Word Bank

easy   Concord
attack   beginning
Paul Revere   night
colonists   Lexington
      redcoats

1. The minutemen wanted to capture the colonists' weapons.

2. Before arriving in Lexington, the British marched all day.

3. The British marched on to Boston after the Battle of Lexington.

4. The British hid along the road, waiting to attack.

5. It was hard to see the British coming in their redcoats.

6. The battles of Lexington and Concord were the end of the Revolutionary War.

Name _____

The Road to Freedom

Read the clues.
Solve the puzzle.

Word Bank
Concord
minutemen
Hancock
Boston
Lexington
Paul Revere
redcoats
Revolutionary
rebels

Down
1. The battles at Lexington and Concord were the start of the _____ War.
2. The first shot of the war was fired in _____.
6. Colonists hid weapons in the town of _____.

Across
1. The British called the colonial soldiers _____.
3. _____ warned the local people that the British were coming.
4. _____ were volunteer soldiers.
5. Lexington and Concord were two towns outside of _____, Massachusetts.
7. John _____ was a patriot leader.
8. Another name for British soldiers was _____.

 **Bonus** Write a coded message from a minuteman in Concord to a patriot in Boston after the Battle of Concord.

THE BATTLE OF BUNKER HILL

The Battle of Bunker Hill was really fought on Breed's Hill.

It was June 1775. Patriots learned that the British were going to occupy the hills over Boston. The Patriot troops wanted to stop them at Bunker Hill. But Breed's Hill was closer to Boston. So that is where the Patriots stood their ground. Colonel William Prescott, their commander, gave them a now-famous order: "Don't one of you fire until you see the whites of their eyes."

Then the British saw that the Patriots had built a fort. They shipped 2,500 soldiers over from Boston. Two times the British troops stormed Breed's Hill. Two times the Patriots forced them to back down. On the third strike, the Patriots ran out of gunpowder. They were forced to retreat. The British took over the hill. This battle was the bloodiest of the Revolutionary War. About 1,000 British and 400 Patriots were either hurt or killed.

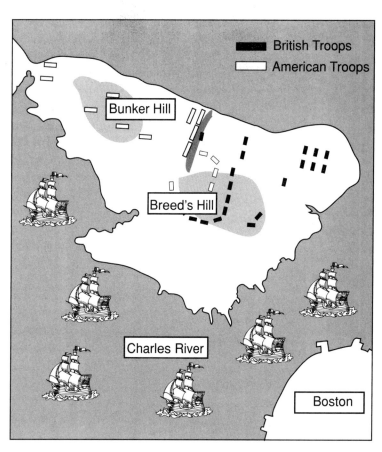

Circle the letter of the best answer.

1. The Battle of Bunker Hill was really fought at _____.
   a. Boston Hill
   b. Breed's Hill
   c. Britain Hill
   d. Rebel Hill

2. The British won the battle on their _____ try.
   a. first
   b. second
   c. third
   d. fourth

3. The _____ did not have enough gunpowder to fight the battle.
   a. British
   b. Patriots
   c. French
   d. Spanish

4. About _____ British and Patriot troops were killed or injured in the battle.
   a. 1,000
   b. 400
   c. 1,400
   d. 10

Name _____

THE BATTLE OF BUNKER HILL

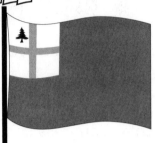

Read each quote.
Decide whether it might have been said by a Patriot or
    a British soldier.
Then color the box in the correct column.

Patriot Soldier	Who Said This?	British Soldier
I	1. We've learned that the British are going to take the hills over Boston. We must beat them to it!	A
E	2. Let's take Bunker Hill before the British get there.	F
R	3. Breed's Hill is closer! Let's stay there.	J
C	4. Look at all the Patriots on Breed's Hill!	D
K	5. We need 2,500 of our soldiers to go over there immediately! We can't let the Patriots win!	L
B	6. Don't one of you fire until you see the whites of their eyes.	T
P	7. Keep attacking those Patriots!	S
H	8. We are running out of gunpowder! We can't fight them off forever!	M
L	9. Retreat! Retreat! We have nothing left to fight with!	N
G	10. We won!	E

Where was the Battle of Bunker Hill really fought?
To answer this question, match each colored letter from above to a numbered line below.

___ ___ ___ ___ ___ ___ ,   ___ ___ ___ ___
 6   3 10   2   4   7   8   1   9   5

 Imagine you that are a soldier fighting in the Battle of Bunker Hill. Write a letter home describing how you feel.

©The Mailbox® • Fascinating Facts: Social Studies • TEC61067 • Key p. 122

Name _____

A New Nation

Thomas Jefferson wrote the Declaration of Independence in about two weeks.

In the summer of 1775, the Second Continental Congress sent a request to the king to help end the war. But he refused to even read the appeal. So the Congress formed an army. It named George Washington to lead the troops.

The Congress also began a move to become independent from England. Its members chose five men to begin work on a paper. The text would tell the world why the colonies should become an independent country. The group agreed that Thomas Jefferson should write the statement of independence.

Jefferson wrote that all men should be equal. He listed the rights that the colonists had not been given by the king. The declaration also said that government should be for the people and that all people have rights.

After Jefferson had worked on the paper for about two weeks, it was ready for the Congress to discuss. On July 4, 1776, it was approved! A new nation was born!

**Unscramble the letters at the end of each sentence to spell a word.
Write the word in the blank.**

1. The colonies tried to make __ __ __ __ __ with the king of England. (eeacp)

2. George Washington became the leader of the __ __ __ __. (yamr)

3. The Declaration of Independence told the __ __ __ __ __ why the colonies should be a separate country. (lwdro)

4. It also stated that people have __ __ __ __ __ __. (grtihs)

5. When the Declaration of Independence was approved, the colonies became a new __ __ __ __ __ __. (tnnoia)

A New Nation

Match each riddle to the correct words on a star.

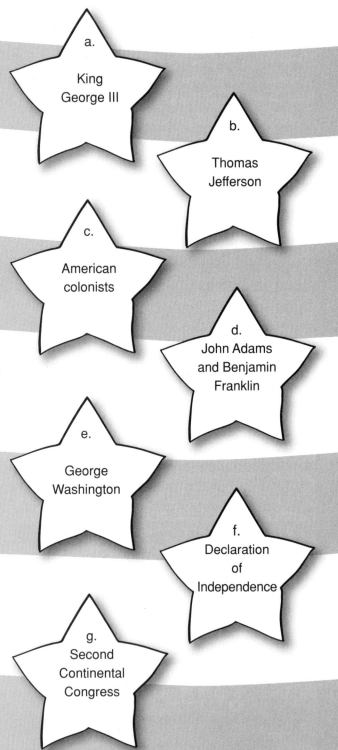

_____ 1. I was chosen with four other men to write a declaration of independence. I wrote it in about two weeks. Who am I?

_____ 2. We met in Philadelphia to declare that the colonies were free and independent of England. Who are we?

_____ 3. Many of us gathered in crowds to hear the Declaration of Independence read aloud. We still had a long, hard fight ahead of us. Who are we?

_____ 4. I explained to the world why the American colonies should separate from Great Britain. What am I?

_____ 5. Those rebel colonists have sent me a request to make peace. I am not going to read it because the Congress that wrote it has no rights. I say that their meeting is not legal. Who am I?

_____ 6. We read the Declaration of Independence after Jefferson finished it. We made a few changes before giving it to the Congress. Who are we?

_____ 7. I have been picked to lead the new Continental army. Who am I?

Stars:
- a. King George III
- b. Thomas Jefferson
- c. American colonists
- d. John Adams and Benjamin Franklin
- e. George Washington
- f. Declaration of Independence
- g. Second Continental Congress

 **Bonus** Imagine that you are a newspaper writer in 1776. Write a news article about the signing of the Declaration of Independence.

Name _____

AN AMERICAN FRONTIERSMAN
Daniel Boone claimed over 100,000 acres of land.

Daniel Boone loved the outdoors. He spent his life hunting and exploring the frontier. His family moved to North Carolina when Daniel was about 16. He hunted and then traded the animal skins for gunpowder, salt, and other items that his family needed.

Daniel once helped a British general on a march through the woods of Pennsylvania. During that march, he met a man who talked about the great hunting land of Kentucky. Daniel wanted to go there. In 1769, he and that same man left for Kentucky. They found a well-worn path used by native people called Warriors' Path. This path led them into Kentucky. Later, he helped connect other trails and buffalo paths. This became known as Wilderness Road. Daniel followed that road to move his family from North Carolina to Kentucky. They settled at a fort he built named Boonesborough.

Daniel became a very rich man in Kentucky. He claimed more than 100,000 acres of land. He lost nearly all of it when he was sued for not getting a title for the land. Daniel later led a group of settlers into Missouri. He died in Missouri in 1820.

**Complete each sentence using a word from the word bank.
Not all words will be used.**

1. Daniel Boone loved the _____.

2. Daniel led his family over the _____ into Kentucky.

3. Daniel claimed over _____ acres of land.

4. The fort that he built was named _____.

5. Daniel died in _____.

Word Bank	
indoors	Kentucky
outdoors	Boonesborough
Missouri	50,000
Wilderness Road	pioneers
Warriors' Path	100,000

AN AMERICAN FRONTIERSMAN

Unscramble the word to complete each sentence.

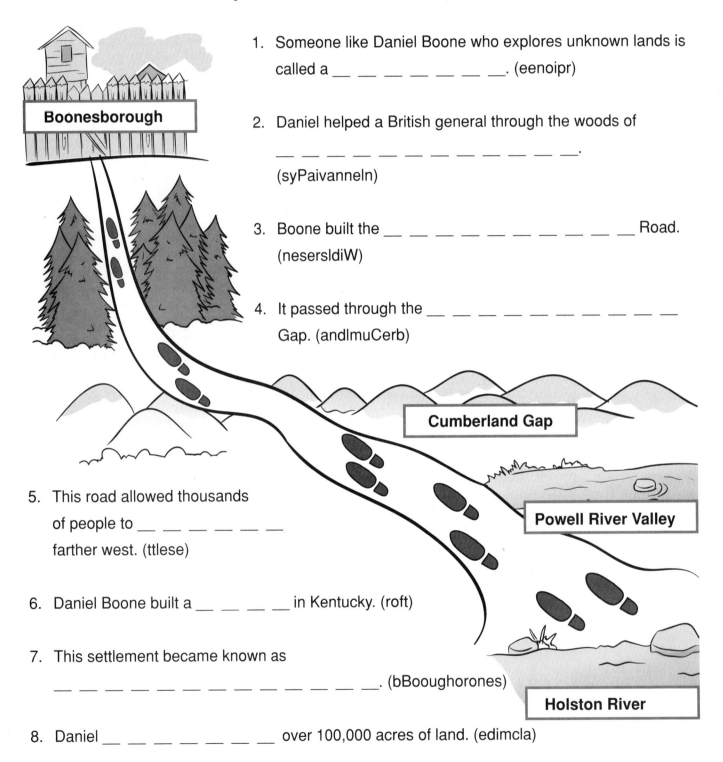

Boonesborough

Cumberland Gap

Powell River Valley

Holston River

1. Someone like Daniel Boone who explores unknown lands is called a __ __ __ __ __ __ __. (eenoipr)

2. Daniel helped a British general through the woods of __ __ __ __ __ __ __ __ __ __ __ __ __ __. (syPaivanneln)

3. Boone built the __ __ __ __ __ __ __ __ __ Road. (nesersldiW)

4. It passed through the __ __ __ __ __ __ __ __ __ __ Gap. (andlmuCerb)

5. This road allowed thousands of people to __ __ __ __ __ __ farther west. (ttlese)

6. Daniel Boone built a __ __ __ __ in Kentucky. (roft)

7. This settlement became known as __ __ __ __ __ __ __ __ __ __ __ __ __ __. (bBooughorones)

8. Daniel __ __ __ __ __ __ __ over 100,000 acres of land. (edimcla)

Bonus Explain why you would or would not like to have lived the life of a pioneer.

©The Mailbox® • Fascinating Facts: Social Studies • TEC61067 • Key p. 122

Making the Deal

The United States bought more than 529 million acres of land for about three cents an acre.

In 1801, many American farmers sent their goods to New Orleans. The items were loaded on boats, taken to other countries, and sold. But France controlled New Orleans.

Thomas Jefferson was president. He wanted the United States to have the land around New Orleans. The Americans could use the port at any time if they owned it. But France's leader said no. Then, in 1802, the port closed to the Americans.

After that, the French were told that the Americans might fight for the port. So on April 30, 1803, France made a deal with the United States. It was called the Louisiana Purchase. The Americans paid France about $15 million for 529 million acres of land and control of New Orleans. Years later, the land was divided to form all or parts of 15 new states.

Complete each sentence.

1. American farmers shipped their _____ to New Orleans.

2. _____ controlled New Orleans.

3. The United States wanted the land around the _____.

4. In 1803, the Americans made a deal with France called the _____

    _____.

5. The Americans paid about _____ for the land.

Making the Deal

Name _____

Cut out the boxes below. Arrange them in the correct order and then glue them to the crates.

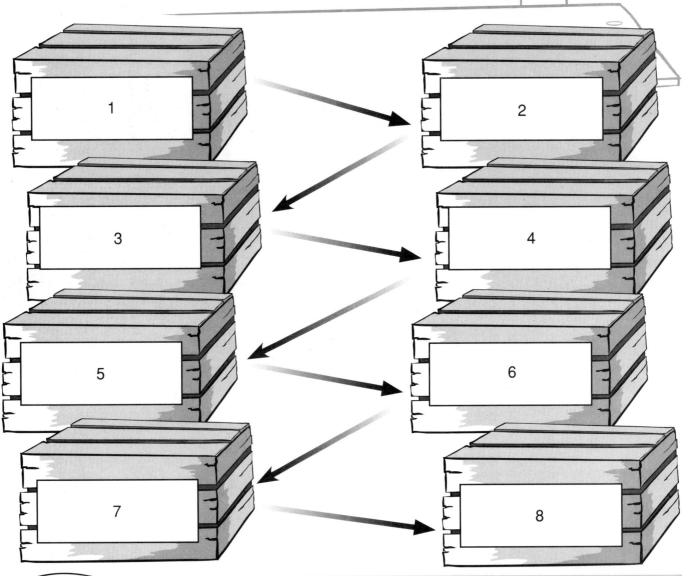

Bonus All or parts of which states were formed from the land bought in the Louisiana Purchase? On the back of this page, list each one and its date of statehood.

©The Mailbox® • *Fascinating Facts: Social Studies* • TEC61067 • Key p. 122

| Farmers ship their goods to New Orleans. | The French are told the Americans might attack. | The United States wants the land around New Orleans. | The Louisiana Purchase is made. |
| The United States gets control of the port. | The French leader refuses to give it up. | Americans can't use the port. | All or parts of 15 new states are formed. |

Name _____

An Incredible Journey

Lewis and Clark traveled about 8,000 miles into the wilderness.

The United States bought the Louisiana Territory in 1803. Little was known about it or the land beyond it. Congress had set aside money to explore the land. Meriwether Lewis was chosen to lead the journey. He asked William Clark to help him. The pair gathered a group of about 31 men. The journey started near St. Louis, Missouri, on May 14, 1804, and ended on September 23, 1806.

The men traveled to the Pacific Ocean and back. They used boats and horses, and also walked. The group had to struggle through rapids and over rocky mountain passes. Harsh weather and a lack of food made the trip hard. Sacagawea and her husband joined the group during the first winter. She was a Native American who helped them talk to tribes.

Clark mapped the journey. Both men wrote about and drew pictures of 178 new plants and 122 new animals. Their journey helped people learn more about the western part of the United States.

Circle the letter of the correct answer.

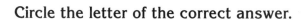

1. Why did Congress want the Louisiana Territory explored?
   a. it was big   b. to find gold   c. little was known about it

2. How long did the trip take?
   a. two weeks   b. two months   c. two years

3. Which of the following did Lewis and Clark not do on their trip?
   a. make maps   b. take pictures   c. talk to Native Americans

4. Which hardship did Lewis and Clark not face?
   a. running out of gas   b. rapids   c. lack of food

5. Their trip was important because it _____.
   a. was challenging   b. took two years   c. uncovered new information about the western United States

Name _____

An Incredible Journey

If the statement is a fact, color the canoe red.
If the statement is an opinion, color the canoe brown.

1 The United States bought the Louisiana Territory in 1803.

2 The United States Congress set aside money to explore the land.

3 Lewis and Clark started and ended their trip near St. Louis.

4 The journey shouldn't have taken as long as it did.

5 For part of the journey, the group followed the river.

6 The trip was harder than it should have been.

7 Lewis and Clark traveled to the Pacific Ocean.

8 The new plants they discovered were beautiful.

9 It is exciting to explore new lands.

10 Sacagawea and her husband helped Lewis and Clark.

11 The explorers had fun keeping journals and drawing pictures.

12 Their journey taught people about the West.

Bonus Pretend that you want to be hired to travel with Lewis and Clark. Write a letter convincing them that you would be a good person to have in their group.

The Bird Woman

Legends say that Sacagawea was a guide, but it is more likely that she was an interpreter.

Sacagawea was from the Shoshone tribe. Her name means "bird woman." When she was a child, she was kidnapped. In time, she was traded to a man who became her husband.

Some say Sacagawea helped Lewis and Clark on their journey across the northwestern United States. Actually, when she was about 16 years old, Sacagawea and her husband were hired as interpreters for the trip. Soon after they began their journey, she gave birth to a son. She carried him with her across the country.

Sacagawea and her husband could speak several languages. This allowed them to talk with the Shoshone and help the group get horses.

Sacagawea died at the age of 25. She is remembered today on stamps, coins, and statues across the country.

Write "true" or "false."

_____ 1. Sacagawea guided Lewis and Clark on their journey.

_____ 2. An interpreter helps people who do not speak the same language understand each other.

_____ 3. Sacagawea's husband kidnapped her at a young age.

_____ 4. Sacagawea never returned to her native land.

_____ 5. Sacagawea died before her son grew into an adult.

_____ 6. Sacagawea remains well known today.

Name _____

The Bird Woman

Color each fact orange.
Color each opinion brown.

1. The bird woman was the best interpreter.

2. Sacagawea was kidnapped as a child.

3. Her husband also traveled with Lewis and Clark.

4. Sacagawea lived the most interesting life of any Shoshone.

5. Sacagawea was the only woman in the group.

6. Sacagawea gave birth to a baby boy while on the trip.

7. Sacagawea made better trades than other explorers.

8. The trip was harder for Sacagawea because she carried her baby boy.

 Imagine what it might have been like for Sacagawea on the trip. Write a journal entry for a day on the trail.

 ©The Mailbox® • Fascinating Facts: Social Studies • TEC61067 • Key p. 123

The Traveling Parchment

A Fort Knox vault guarded the Constitution during World War II.

The Constitution began its long journey the day after its signing. First, it was taken by stagecoach to the U.S. Congress in New York. In 1800, it was moved to Washington, DC, when government offices were moved to the new capital. To get there, the papers sailed by ship and were housed in quite a few places. During the War of 1812, the capital was attacked. The papers were placed in linen sacks and moved by carts to an unused mill.

In 1921, the Constitution was carried in a Model T Ford to its new home at the Library of Congress. After the attack on Pearl Harbor, it was moved again. A train rushed the Constitution to Fort Knox, Kentucky. It remained there through most of World War II. Then, in 1952, the Constitution was moved to its final home. Inside an armored truck, the parchment was placed on mattresses. It was escorted to the National Archives Building in Washington, DC. What a voyage!

Match the Constitution's home to its method of travel.

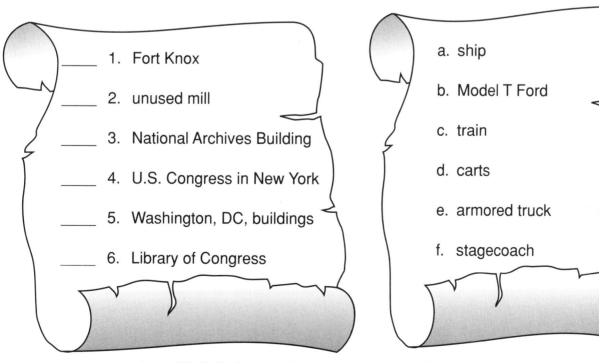

_____ 1. Fort Knox

_____ 2. unused mill

_____ 3. National Archives Building

_____ 4. U.S. Congress in New York

_____ 5. Washington, DC, buildings

_____ 6. Library of Congress

a. ship

b. Model T Ford

c. train

d. carts

e. armored truck

f. stagecoach

The Traveling Parchment

Read the clues.
Solve the puzzle.

Across

4. The place where the Constitution was sent to after its signing was

    _____ _____.

5. During the War of 1812, the Constitution was placed in linen _____. It was then moved to an unused mill.

8. The Constitution has been housed in many buildings in _____, the capital of the United States.

9. When the mill was in danger, _____ were used to move the Constitution to an empty house.

Down

1. At the Library of Congress, the Constitution was kept in a marble, bronze, and glass _____.

2. After the attack on _____ _____, the Constitution was taken by train to Fort Knox.

3. Now, when not on display, the Constitution is lowered into a safe _____.

6. The first four pages of the Constitution are displayed together only on September 17 each year. This day is called _____ Day.

7. The current home of the Constitution is the National _____ Building.

Word Bank
Archives
case
Constitution
New York
Pearl Harbor
sacks
vault
wagons
Washington, DC

Bonus Why do you think the United States wants to protect the Constitution? Write a paragraph explaining your thoughts.

Name _____   **James Madison**

A GREAT LITTLE MAN

James Madison is known as the Father of the Constitution.

In 1787, a group of 55 men came to Philadelphia and wrote a constitution. James Madison arrived first. He had to wait several days for many of the others. But once the meeting began, he took notes every day! Before long, he was called the Great Little Madison for his hard work. The name fit. At only five feet four inches tall and about 100 pounds, he was quite small for a grown man!

After the Constitution was signed, Madison returned to Montpelier, the name of his home in Virginia. There he was elected to the U.S. House of Representatives. Later, he also served the young country as secretary of state. In 1809, Madison became the fourth, and shortest, president of the United States.

Madison's journals of the Constitutional Convention were not made public until after his death. Congress bought them for $30,000. His notes were published. Now all Americans can read the words spoken by the founders of the nation.

Write a word from the word bank to complete each sentence.

1. Congress bought Madison's _____ for $30,000.

2. James Madison was the _____ president in U.S. history.

3. Because he worked hard at the Constitutional Convention, Madison became known as the _____ of the Constitution.

4. The Constitutional Convention met in _____.

5. Madison was _____ as the country's fourth president.

6. The house in Virginia where James Madison lived is called _____.

Word Bank
Montpelier
elected
journals
Father
Philadelphia
shortest

©The Mailbox® • *Fascinating Facts: Social Studies* • TEC61067 • Key p. 123   **39**

A GREAT LITTLE MAN

Unscramble the letters to spell each missing word.

1. James Madison's home state was _ _ _ _ _ _ _ _. (griVnaii)

2. As a child, James was often _ _ _ _. (ikcs)

3. Madison's home in Virginia was called _ _ _ _ _ _ _ _ _ _ _. (peiMonlert)

4. Thomas _ _ _ _ _ _ _ _ was Madison's close friend. (nJrofefes)

5. During the Constitutional Convention, James Madison took _ _ _ _ _ daily. (tsneo)

6. All records at the convention were kept _ _ _ _ _ _. (terces)

7. Madison helped write the Bill of _ _ _ _ _ _. (gsRtih)

8. Madison married _ _ _ _ _ _ Payne Todd. (loDyel)

9. In 1809, Madison became the _ _ _ _ _ _ U.S. president. (rutfoh)

10. While president, Madison led the country during the _ _ _ of 1812. (rWa)

 What do you think was James Madison's most vital role in the early years of the country? Explain.

SIGN HERE

Delegates signed the Constitution in geographic order from north to south.

The U.S. Constitution was signed on September 17, 1787. There were 55 delegates at the Constitutional Convention. Only 39 of them signed the Constitution. They all played a big role in forming the Constitution. But it was Gouverneur Morris who wrote it. He wrote all the decisions in a revised form.

The delegates debated and discussed the Constitution for four months. Then the Constitution was finished. The 39 delegates took turns signing the document. They signed in geographic order from north to south. William Jackson witnessed the signing. They all hoped they had planned a strong national government. They hoped at least nine states would approve it.

Circle the letter of the best answer.

1. How many people signed the Constitution?
   a. 55
   b. 39
   c. 17

2. Who wrote the Constitution down on paper?
   a. George Washington
   b. William Jackson
   c. Gouverneur Morris

3. In what order was the Constitution signed?
   a. alphabetical
   b. geographical
   c. numerical

4. Who witnessed the signing of the Constitution?
   a. George Washington
   b. William Jackson
   c. Gouverneur Morris

SIGN HERE

Use the code to reveal some facts about the signers of the U.S. Constitution.

1. At 81, he was the oldest person to sign the Constitution.

   __ __ __ __ __ __ __ __   __ __ __ __ __ __ __ __
   2 5 14 10 1 13 9 14   6 17 1 14 11 12 9 14

2. At 26, he was the youngest person to sign the Constitution.

   __ __ __ __ __ __ __ __   __ __ __ __ __ __
   10 15 14 1 19 8 1 14   4 1 21 19 15 14

3. He was the first person to sign the Constitution.

   __ __ __ __ __ __   __ __ __ __ __ __ __ __ __ __
   7 5 15 17 7 5   20 1 18 8 9 14 7 19 15 14

4. This state did not have any signatures on the Constitution.

   __ __ __ __ __   __ __ __ __ __ __
   17 8 15 4 5   9 18 12 1 14 4

5. This is the name of the building where the Constitution was signed.

   __ __ __ __ __ __ __ __ __ __ __ __   __ __ __ __
   9 14 4 5 16 5 14 4 5 14 3 5   8 1 12 12

6. These two signers became U.S. presidents.

   __ __ __ __ __ __ __   and   __ __ __ __ __ __ __ __ __ __
   13 1 4 9 18 15 14   20 1 18 8 9 14 7 19 15 14

7. Six of the men who signed the Constitution also signed this document.

   __ __ __ __ __ __ __ __ __ __ __   __ __
   4 5 3 12 1 17 1 19 9 15 14   15 6

   __ __ __ __ __ __ __ __ __ __ __ __
   9 14 4 5 16 5 14 4 5 14 3 5

Code

A	B	C	D	E	F	G	H	I	J	K	L	M	N	O	P	R	S	T	W	Y
1	2	3	4	5	6	7	8	9	10	11	12	13	14	15	16	17	18	19	20	21

Bonus Use a reference book to find the names of the six men in statement 7.

©The Mailbox® • Fascinating Facts: Social Studies • TEC61067 • Key p. 123

Freedoms and Rights

North Carolina and Rhode Island would not approve the U.S. Constitution without a bill of rights.

After the Constitutional Convention of 1787, some people still felt that the U.S. Constitution needed something more. They thought it needed a bill of rights to protect people's freedoms. In fact, two states refused to approve the Constitution without this change.

James Madison led Congress in creating such a document. He looked at more than 100 ideas! He chose 15 that he thought were the most vital. Madison presented these to Congress.

After much debate, 12 amendments were sent to the states for approval. It took the states two years to decide! At last, ten of the 12 amendments were confirmed and added to the Constitution. These ten amendments became law on December 15, 1791. The Bill of Rights became part of the Constitution!

Color a parchment to show whether each sentence is true or false.

True	False	
		1. It took the states less than two years to accept the Bill of Rights.
		2. James Madison helped form the Bill of Rights.
		3. The Bill of Rights became part of the U.S. Constitution at the Constitutional Convention.
		4. The states approved 12 amendments.
		5. Some states would not approve the Constitution without the Bill of Rights.
		6. The Bill of Rights is a permanent part of the Constitution.

Freedoms and Rights

Read each statement.
Write the matching amendment number that supports each statement.
Not all amendments will be used.
Some amendments will be used more than once.

___ A. Police believe you have a stolen car in your garage. They cannot search for it without a warrant.

___ B. The army cannot put a soldier in your home, without your permission.

___ C. You cannot be assigned a church to attend.

___ D. A man is accused of a crime. He cannot be put in jail for ten years before a trial.

___ E. Police officers carry weapons.

___ F. Each state sets its own rules about when a person can get a driver's license.

___ G. An accused thief is arrested. He refuses to answer any questions.

___ H. A group of your neighbors carry signs to protest an increase in taxes.

___ I. The newspaper prints a story about a mayor who gets a ticket for speeding.

Amendment 1
Freedom of speech
Freedom of religion
Freedom of the press
Freedom of assembly

Amendment 2
Right to keep and bear arms

Amendment 3
Prevents a homeowner from being required to house a soldier

Amendment 4
Protects a person from having his home searched without a warrant

Amendment 5
Protects a person from having to witness against himself
Prevents a person from being charged twice for the same crime

Amendment 6
Right to a fair trial

Amendment 7
Right to a trial by jury in a civil case of more than $20

Amendment 8
Right to fair bail, fines, and punishment

Amendment 9
Protects other rights not mentioned in the Bill of Rights

Amendment 10
Any powers not given to the federal government belong to the states

BONUS Choose one amendment from the Bill of Rights. Write about a situation that is allowed by the amendment. Then write about a situation that is not allowed by the amendment.

©The Mailbox® • *Fascinating Facts: Social Studies* • TEC61067 • Key p. 123

SHARED DUTIES

Only the federal government can print money.

Before the U.S. Constitution, the Articles of Confederation were the law of the land. Each state made its own laws. States governed themselves. The national government had little power. The public had lived under England's control. The people recalled what life was like before the Revolutionary War. Therefore, they wanted the states to hold most of the power. But leaders saw a need for a more powerful central government. It needed a leading role. Without that, the new nation would be weak. After the Constitution was signed, the federal government became stronger.

Today, the work of the nation is shared. There are many duties. The federal government can print money and declare war. But states also have a vital role. They govern schools and conduct elections. Both can collect taxes. The federal and state governments work jointly, sharing the duties of government.

Circle the letter of the best answer.

1. What was the first set of laws after the Revolutionary War called?
   a. the U.S. Constitution
   b. the Articles of Confederation
   c. the national government

2. How is the Constitution different from the Articles of Confederation?
   a. The Constitution created a strong central government.
   b. The Articles of Confederation gave the states little power.
   c. The Articles of Confederation were made by the British. The Constitution was made by the United States.

3. The federal government has the power to _____.
   a. establish schools
   b. print money
   c. take power from the states

4. What is the main idea of this passage?
   a. The Articles of Confederation were not good laws.
   b. The U.S. Constitution is the law of today.
   c. The state and federal governments share the tasks of government.

Federal and state governments

SHARED DUTIES

Cut apart the cards below.
Glue each card in the correct section.

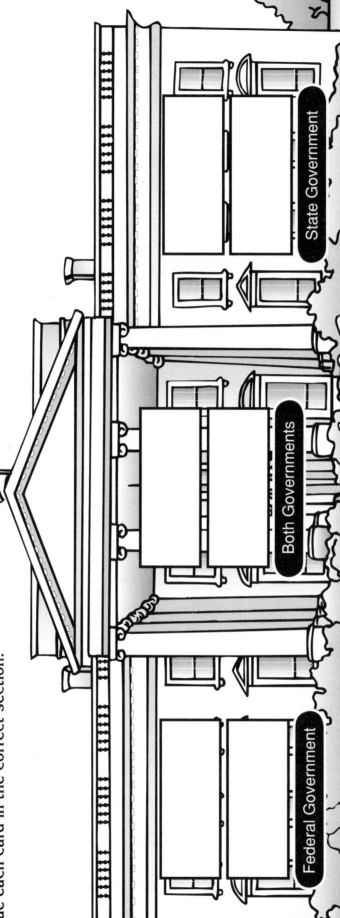

State Government

Both Governments

Federal Government

BONUS What do you think life would be like in the United States if the Articles of Confederation were still the law of the land?

©The Mailbox® • *Fascinating Facts: Social Studies* • TEC61067 • Key p. 124

| makes treaties | conducts elections | make and enforce laws | issues driver's licenses | sets up post offices | build roads |

THE COUNTRY'S LEADER

At 42 years of age, Theodore Roosevelt was the country's youngest president.

Who is the leader of the executive branch? The president is! He is elected for four years. The president must be at least 35 years old. He has to have lived in the country for 14 years and be a natural-born citizen.

The president must fulfill many duties. He ensures that federal laws are followed and makes treaties with foreign countries. Being the armed forces leader is a big duty for the head of state. As problems arise, the president can suggest laws to Congress. When a bill is passed, he can sign it into law or veto it.

The president does not do all the work of the executive branch. The vice president and other cabinet members help him. If something happens to the president, the vice president would take over. It takes many people to do the work of the executive branch.

Color a star to show whether each sentence is true or false.

True	False
☆	☆
☆	☆
☆	☆
☆	☆
☆	☆
☆	☆

1. The president is elected for ten years.

2. The president can make laws.

3. The president is the leader of the armed forces.

4. Congress would take over if the president died.

5. The vice president is a part of the executive branch.

6. If the president signs a bill, it becomes a law.

THE COUNTRY'S LEADER

Cut out the cards. Glue each card to its matching fact. If you are correct, your answers will spell out the name of the group the president suggests laws to.

1. The 22nd Amendment was added to the Constitution in this year. It states that a president can be elected only twice.

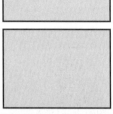

2. The president takes the oath of office on this day in January.

3. This is the annual salary of the president.

4. The president's cabinet heads this many federal departments.

5. This is the number of presidents who were born in the state of Virginia.

6. John F. Kennedy was the president to live the shortest life. He died at this age.

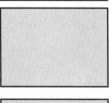

7. This is the number of presidents who have died on the Fourth of July.

8. After only one month as president, William H. Harrison died. This is the year he died.

What traits do you think are needed in a person who would like to become president? Explain.

©The Mailbox® • Fascinating Facts: Social Studies • TEC61067 • Key p. 124

C	O	S	N	G	S	R	E
1951	20	three	$400,000	15	1841	eight	46

REPRESENTATIVES FROM EVERY STATE

The first Congress had only 91 members. Now there are 535.

The federal legislative branch created by the U.S. Constitution has the right to make, get rid of, and change laws. The two chambers present up to 10,000 bills during a two-year term. But only about 600 bills are signed into law.

The two-house Congress is part of the U.S. Constitution. In the Senate, each state has an equal number of senators. This chamber consists of two members from each state. Each member serves a six-year term. The House of Representatives is based on the number of people in the state. Each of these 435 members is elected for two years. Each legislator is elected by the people of her state.

All 535 members of Congress meet in the Capitol in Washington, DC. This building is known as a symbol of the legislative branch of the U.S. government.

Make each statement true.
Cross out the word that does not belong.
Write a word from the word bank above it.

1. The legislative branch has three parts.

2. Every senator serves a two-year term.

3. A state's number of members in the House of Representatives is based on the state's number of cities.

4. A member of Congress is elected by people who live in another state.

5. Senators have a shorter term in office than representatives.

Word Bank
six
longer
her
two
people

REPRESENTATIVES FROM EVERY STATE

Unscramble the letters to complete each sentence.
Circle the answers in the puzzle.

1. A senator is elected by the _ _ _ _ _ _ from a state. (sovret)

2. There is no _ _ _ _ _ on the number of years a member of Congress can serve. (iilmt)

3. The two-house Congress was formed during the Constitutional Convention. It was known

   as the Great _ _ _ _ _ _ _ _ _ _ _. (pmseCimoro)

4. The U.S. legislative branch is located on _ _ _ _ _ _ _ _ _ _ _. (polCtia liHl)

5. The Statue of _ _ _ _ _ _ _ stands on the dome of the Capitol. (meerdoF)

6. Congress's main job is to _ _ _ _ _ _ _ _. (kaem slaw)

L	A	C	S	W	D	R	S	B	F	Q	G
D	K	F	R	Y	J	G	V	W	R	M	V
K	L	I	M	I	T	J	O	I	A	P	F
H	B	E	T	U	Z	A	T	K	E	J	Y
F	N	V	U	N	K	M	E	S	I	N	K
O	R	Y	C	O	C	L	R	C	A	E	D
P	G	E	Q	Z	A	H	S	V	L	I	V
A	X	L	E	W	X	Q	F	I	T	J	X
H	Q	T	S	D	G	W	T	O	M	D	M
L	L	I	H	L	O	T	I	P	A	C	W
M	H	E	C	B	L	M	P	S	N	Z	B
U	W	C	O	M	P	R	O	M	I	S	E

Bonus Why do you think the writers of the Constitution split Congress into two parts? Explain.

©The Mailbox® • *Fascinating Facts: Social Studies* • TEC61067 • Key p. 124

ORDER IN THE COURTS!

Since 1803, the Supreme Court has ruled that over 1,000 laws were unconstitutional.

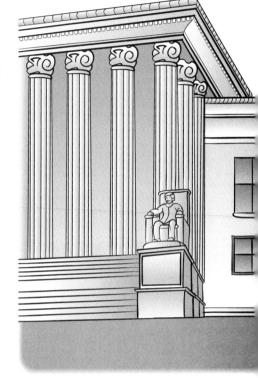

Laws are rules that everyone has to follow. The judicial branch of our government is made up of courts and judges. The courts make sure that the laws are used fairly. They also make sure that the laws follow the U.S. Constitution. The highest court in our country is the Supreme Court. There are nine judges on the Supreme Court. They have the final say about a law. If they rule a law is unconstitutional, then the rest of the courts in the country must follow their decision. Since 1803, the Supreme Court has ruled that over 1,000 laws were unconstitutional.

Write a word or words from the word bank to complete each sentence.

1. Laws are _____ that everyone must follow.

2. Courts are part of the _____ branch.

3. The _____ Court is the highest court in our country.

4. There are _____ judges on the Supreme Court.

5. The Supreme Court's job is to make sure the laws are used _____ and

   follow the _____.

Word Bank

nine	Constitution	fairly
rules	judicial	Supreme

ORDER IN THE COURTS!

Match each word to its definition.

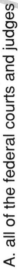

_____ 1. amendment

_____ 2. Bill of Rights

_____ 3. due process of law

_____ 4. jury

_____ 5. dispute

_____ 6. judicial branch

_____ 7. interpret

_____ 8. Supreme Court

_____ 9. unconstitutional

_____ 10. judicial review

A. all of the federal courts and judges

B. the highest court in the United States

C. the process that gives a person a fair trial

D. a change in the Constitution

E. against the Constitution

F. the basic rights of all people

G. to explain the meaning of a law

H. the power of a court to rule a law as unconstitutional

I. a group of people who decide a verdict in a trial

J. an argument

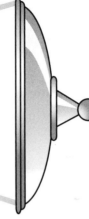

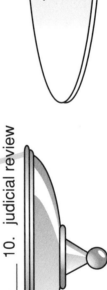

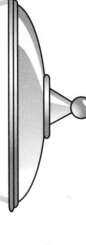

Bonus

Explain how the judicial branch plays a role in the system of checks and balances in government.

©The Mailbox® • *Fascinating Facts: Social Studies* • TEC61067 • Key p. 124

KEEPING IT IN BALANCE

Only about 4 percent of all vetoed bills have been overridden by Congress.

If one person has all the power, he can make all the choices. When the United States was founded, leaders did not want this for the country. So the U.S. Constitution divided the government into three branches. The Legislative Branch was given the duty of making laws. The task of enforcing the laws belonged to the executive branch. Interpreting laws became the job of the judicial branch. But the writers of the Constitution went a step further. A system was formed so that each branch had the power to check the others.

For instance, Congress can pass a bill. Then the president can sign it into law or veto it. If he vetoes the bill, it can still become a law. Congress can override the veto with a two-thirds majority vote. Also, any bill signed into law can be ruled unconstitutional by the Supreme Court.

Read each statement. Decide whether it is true always, sometimes, or never. Then circle the correct scale.

Always	Sometimes	Never	
⚖	⚖	⚖	1. The president signs bills into law.
⚖	⚖	⚖	2. Congress makes laws.
⚖	⚖	⚖	3. The Supreme Court rules on whether laws are constitutional.
⚖	⚖	⚖	4. The judicial branch can override a president's veto.
⚖	⚖	⚖	5. Each branch of government has the duty to check on the other two.
⚖	⚖	⚖	6. Congress passes vetoed bills into laws.

54

KEEPING IT IN BALANCE

Cut out the boxes below.
Glue each one under the correct branch.

EXECUTIVE BRANCH

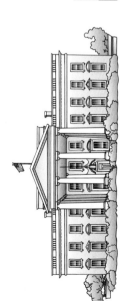

LEGISLATIVE BRANCH

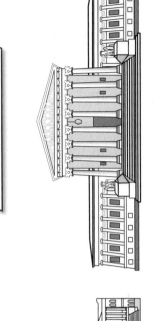

JUDICIAL BRANCH

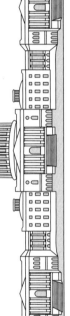

Bonus Why do you think presidents were cautioned to rarely use the veto power? Explain.

| can impeach a president or vice president | writes the nation's budget | must approve all Supreme Court appointments | can rule that a decision made by the president is unconstitutional | appoints Supreme Court justices | decides the meaning of laws |

Every Vote Counts!

Only about half of the people signed up to vote really do vote.

Americans have been voting since the founding of our country. To vote, one must be at least 18 years old. One must also be a U.S. citizen. People vote on many different issues. But only about half the number of voters go to cast a ballot. Sometimes the number of votes is very close. In 1994, two candidates received the same number of votes for a seat in the Wyoming House of Representatives. To break the tie, the two candidates' names were written on Ping-Pong balls. The Ping-Pong balls were dropped in a cowboy hat. Randall Luthi's name was drawn. He won the election for a seat in the state House of Representatives.

Make each statement true. Cross out the word that does not belong. Write a word from the word bank above it. Not all words will be used.

1. To vote in the United States, one must be at least 21 years old.

2. Only U.S. tourists can vote in a U.S. election.

3. Americans have been voting since the founding of Canada.

4. People vote on many different votes.

5. The number of votes is never close.

| **Word Bank** |
| the United States |
| France |
| issues |
| rules |
| sometimes |
| always |
| citizens |
| prisoners |
| 18 |
| 16 |

Every Vote Counts!

Use the timeline below to solve the puzzle.

1. In the late _____, computers were used for voting.
2. _____ cards were first used in the early 1960s.
3. In 1892, the _____ lever voting machine was used.
4. The Voting Rights Act kept states from using _____ voting rules.
5. The 15th Amendment gave citizens of all _____ the right to vote.
6. The first _____ ballots were used in 1629.
7. The Electoral _____ elects the president and vice president.
8. The 19th Amendment gave women the right to _____.

What word is used to describe a person's right to vote?
To answer the question, write the word formed in the boldfaced boxes.

_ _ _ _ _ _ _ _ _

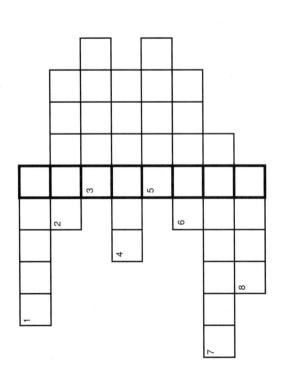

VOTING TIMELINE

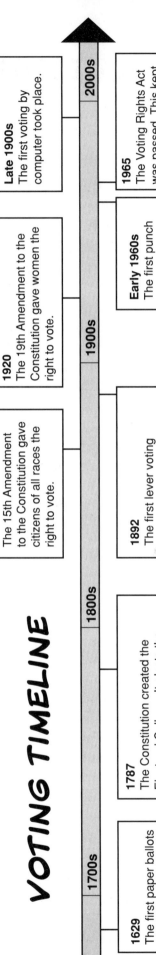

1700s

1629
The first paper ballots were used.

1787
The Constitution created the Electoral College. It elects the president and vice president of the United States.

1800s

1870
The 15th Amendment to the Constitution gave citizens of all races the right to vote.

1892
The first lever voting machine was used instead of paper ballots.

1900s

1920
The 19th Amendment to the Constitution gave women the right to vote.

Early 1960s
The first punch cards were used for voting.

1965
The Voting Rights Act was passed. This kept states from using unfair voting rules.

Late 1900s
The first voting by computer took place.

2000s

Bonus

Research the Voting Rights Act. Explain why it came about even though the 15th Amendment already gave minorities the right to vote.

©The Mailbox® • *Fascinating Facts: Social Studies* • TEC61067 • Key p. 124

A Promise of Loyalty

The wording of the Pledge of Allegiance has been changed three times!

In 1892, the United States honored the 400th anniversary of Christopher Columbus's first trip to the Americas. *The Youth's Companion,* a magazine for children, printed a short pledge to help make it an extra special day. Francis Bellamy wrote the famous pledge. He also sent it in a leaflet throughout the country. He asked schools to fly the flag and promote citizenship among the children. More than 12 million schoolchildren said the pledge on Columbus Day, October 12, 1892. Since that time, the pledge has become an American tradition.

The pledge has changed over the years. In 1923 and 1924, the words *my flag* were changed to *the flag of the United States of America.* The pledge became the country's official pledge when it was added to the flag code in 1942. Its last change occurred in 1954 when the words *under God* became a part of this patriotic promise.

I pledge allegiance to my Flag, and to the Republic for which it stands: one Nation indivisible, With Liberty and Justice for all.

Answer each question in a complete sentence.

1. Why was the Pledge of Allegiance written? _____

   _____

2. How did children and schools find out about the Columbus Day celebration? _____

   _____

3. How do we know that the celebration was a success? _____

   _____

4. How has the Pledge of Allegiance changed? _____

   _____

Name _____

A Promise of Loyalty

Match each word to its definition.

_____ 1. pledge

_____ 2. allegiance

_____ 3. republic

_____ 4. indivisible

_____ 5. liberty

_____ 6. justice

A. freedom

B. nation

C. promise

D. fairness

E. undivided

F. loyalty

I pledge allegiance to the flag of the United States of America and to the republic for which it stands, one nation under God, indivisible, with liberty and justice for all.

Bonus How do you think the Pledge of Allegiance might be changed in the future? Explain.

©The Mailbox® • *Fascinating Facts: Social Studies* • TEC61067 • Key p. 125

Name _____

Old Glory

The 50-star American flag was designed by a 17-year-old for a school project!

In 1958, Robert Heft designed a new U.S. flag. It had 50 stars on it. The old flag had 48. Two new states would be added to the Union. It took 12½ hours to create the flag. Then Robert turned it in for a grade. His teacher gave him a B–. He thought Robert's flag was unoriginal. Robert convinced his teacher to change the grade if he could get Congress to accept his design.

Robert sent the flag to Walter Moeller, his congressman. Moeller got Robert's design approved by Congress. Robert's teacher raised his grade. Since then, Robert's original flag has flown over every state capitol. It is also the only flag to fly over the White House under five different presidents.

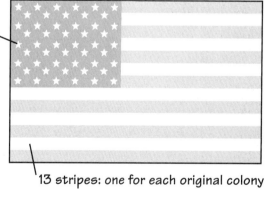

50 stars: one for each state

13 stripes: one for each original colony

Number the sentences below in the correct order.

____ Robert's teacher changed his grade.

____ Robert spent 12½ hours making his flag.

____ Robert's teacher gave him a B–.

____ Robert Heft designed a new flag.

____ Robert's congressman got Congress to approve his new design.

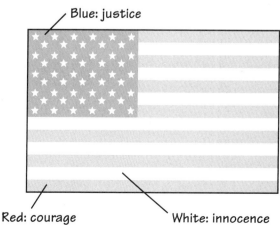

Blue: justice

Red: courage   White: innocence

Old Glory

Below are some guidelines for the American flag.
Write each rule number on the matching flag.

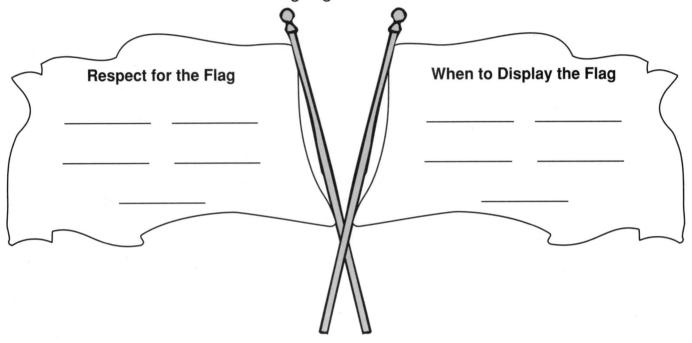

Respect for the Flag

_____ _____

_____ _____

_____

When to Display the Flag

_____ _____

_____ _____

_____

1. Display the flag from sunrise to sunset.

2. The flag should be displayed at polls on election days.

3. Never use the flag to carry or hold something.

4. The flag cannot be used as a decorative cover on a ceiling.

5. Display the flag during school days in every school.

6. Do not use the flag for any type of advertising.

7. The flag should not be printed on anything that is meant to be thrown away.

8. The flag should be displayed on all days, especially holidays such as Flag Day and Veterans Day.

9. Unless you are using an all-weather flag, do not display the flag on rainy or snowy days.

10. Do not display or store the flag in a way that it can get damaged.

 **Research the Flag Protection Act of 1989. Explain what it is and why it was created.**

Name_____

Patriotic Song

"The Star-Spangled Banner" became the national anthem
117 years after it was written.

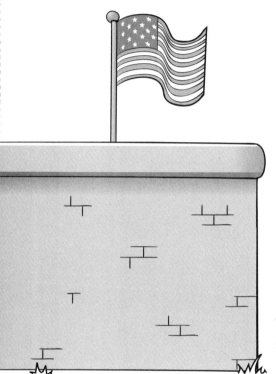

Many countries have a special song called a national anthem. The United States's anthem is about our country's flag.

America was at war with Great Britain in 1814. On September 13, a British ship attacked Fort McHenry in Maryland. An American named Francis Scott Key was near the fort. He watched bombs hit the fort during the night. He worried that the British might take control of the fort. When the sun came up, the American flag was still flying high! Key was so excited that he wrote a poem about the event.

The poem was published in Baltimore. A note explained that it should be sung to a tune that was popular at that time. Soon the song was printed in other cities. People liked it. In 1895, the U.S. Army decided to sing it each day when it raised and lowered the flag. Then, in 1931, Congress declared "The Star-Spangled Banner" the United States's national anthem.

Complete each sentence. Use the passage.

1. "The Star-Spangled Banner" is about the American _____.

2. In 1814, America was at war with _____ _____.

3. The British attacked _____ _____ in Maryland.

4. Francis Scott Key wrote a _____ about the battle.

5. In 1931, "The Star-Spangled Banner" became the national _____.

Name _____

Patriotic Song

If the statement is a fact, color the star red.
If the statement is an opinion, color the star blue.

 1. Francis Scott Key was a great American.

 2. Key wrote "The Star-Spangled Banner" about the American flag.

 3. America was at war with Great Britain in 1814.

 4. The British attack on Fort McHenry wasn't a wise decision.

 5. Francis Scott Key shouldn't have worried that the fort could fall.

 6. Key's poem was published in many cities.

 7. The poem could be sung to a popular tune.

 8. "The Star-Spangled Banner" is the best song ever written about America.

 9. Today, the song is sung at major sports events.

 10. Congress should have made the song the national anthem much sooner.

 Some people think "God Bless America" should be our national anthem instead of "The Star-Spangled Banner." What do you think? List five reasons on the back of this page to explain your choice.

Name _____

Strong and Proud

Benjamin Franklin wanted the turkey to be the national symbol of the United States.

When the United States was formed, its leaders wanted a national symbol. Benjamin Franklin wanted a North American turkey to be the national symbol. But others felt that the bald eagle was a better choice. They thought eagles were brave, strong, and proud. Benjamin Franklin thought eagles were a bad symbol for the country. He said they stole food from other animals and were lazy. Both the bald eagle and North American turkey are found only in North America. But the people wanted the bald eagle. In 1782, Congress made the bald eagle the national symbol of the United States.

Over two hundred years later, the bald eagle is still a national treasure. Its picture can be found on everything from money to state seals. It is a powerful symbol of the United States.

Make each statement true. Cross out the word that does not belong. Write a word from the passage above it.

1. Benjamin Franklin wanted the eagle to be our national symbol.

2. People thought the bald eagle was a weak bird.

3. In 1782, Franklin made the bald eagle a national symbol.

4. The bald eagle's picture can be found on money and state buttons.

5. The bald eagle is a weak symbol.

Name _____

Strong and Proud

Write the letter of each statement under the correct heading.

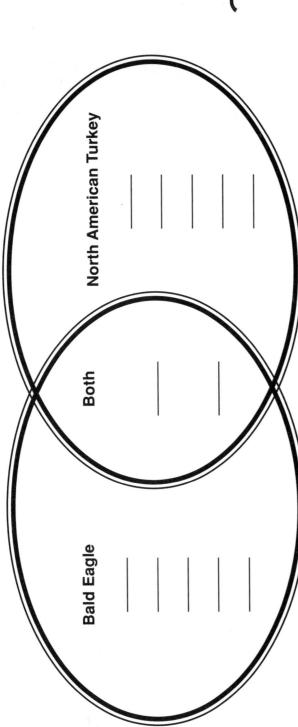

Bald Eagle

Both

North American Turkey

A. Congress wanted the bald eagle to be the national symbol.
B. Benjamin Franklin wanted the North American turkey to be the national symbol.
C. Bald eagles and North American turkeys are found only in North America.
D. Bald eagles live mostly in the United States and Canada.
E. North American turkeys live mostly in the United States and Mexico.
F. Both turkeys and eagles build nests for their young.

G. North American turkeys build their nests on the ground.
H. Bald eagles build their nests in treetops or on cliffs.
I. Bald eagles have strong legs, feet, and talons.
J. Bald eagles will eat whatever meat is easiest to get.
K. North American turkeys eat seeds, insects, and fruits.
L. Male North American turkeys have wattles, or loose pieces of skin under their beaks.

 **BONUS** Which do you think makes a better national symbol: the bald eagle or the North American turkey? Explain.

©The Mailbox® • *Fascinating Facts: Social Studies* • TEC61067 • Key p. 125

Dome of Freedom

The dome over the Capitol's Rotunda weighs almost nine million pounds!

The U.S. Capitol is the home of Congress. But it is much more than just a building for lawmakers. It is a symbol of freedom. The easy-to-recognize cast-iron dome holds the Statue of Freedom. Perched on top of the dome, this woman with a sword and shield welcomes thousands of people each day. Inside the building, the Rotunda's ceiling is decorated with a fresco of George Washington. The curved walls hold paintings and sculptures of famous people and events in U.S. history.

Under the Rotunda, a crypt was built after the death of George Washington. It was built to be the place where he would be buried. He had died at his Mount Vernon home and was buried there. After the crypt was complete, his family did not want his corpse moved. Today, people visit the crypt to see its many displays.

Color a dome to show whether each sentence is true or false.

True	False

1. The Statue of Freedom stands inside the Capitol Rotunda.

2. The Capitol building is a symbol of freedom.

3. The U.S. Senate and the House of Representatives meet in the Capitol.

4. George Washington wanted to be buried in the Capitol.

5. Today, the crypt is off limits to the public.

6. Building a crypt for George Washington began long before his death.

Name _____

66

Dome of Freedom

Write the names of six famous Americans with a statue in Statuary Hall, which is located in the U.S. Capitol. Use the code.

Code

1 = M
2 = U
3 = I
4 = A
5 = D
6 = W
7 = R
8 = E
9 = T
10 = B
11 = J
12 = O
13 = L
14 = G
15 = S
16 = H
17 = N
18 = F

1. $\overline{15}\ \overline{4}\ \overline{1}\ \overline{2}\ \overline{8}\ \overline{13}$
   $\overline{4}\ \overline{5}\ \overline{4}\ \overline{1}\ \overline{15}$

2. $\overline{11}\ \overline{4}\ \overline{1}\ \overline{8}\ \overline{15}$
   $\overline{14}\ \overline{4}\ \overline{7}\ \overline{18}\ \overline{3}\ \overline{8}\ \overline{13}\ \overline{5}$

3. $\overline{15}\ \overline{4}\ \overline{1}$
   $\overline{16}\ \overline{12}\ \overline{2}\ \overline{15}\ \overline{9}\ \overline{12}\ \overline{17}$

4. $\overline{6}\ \overline{3}\ \overline{13}\ \overline{13}$
   $\overline{7}\ \overline{12}\ \overline{14}\ \overline{8}\ \overline{7}\ \overline{15}$

5. $\overline{8}\ \overline{9}\ \overline{16}\ \overline{4}\ \overline{17}$
   $\overline{4}\ \overline{13}\ \overline{13}\ \overline{8}\ \overline{17}$

6. $\overline{7}\ \overline{12}\ \overline{10}\ \overline{8}\ \overline{7}\ \overline{9}$
   $\overline{18}\ \overline{2}\ \overline{13}\ \overline{9}\ \overline{12}\ \overline{17}$

BONUS If you could add a statue of a famous American to Statuary Hall, of whom would it be? Explain.

©The Mailbox® • Fascinating Facts: Social Studies • TEC61067 • Key p. 125

Name _____

 Washington Monument

Remembering a President

The Washington Monument is the tallest stone structure in the world.

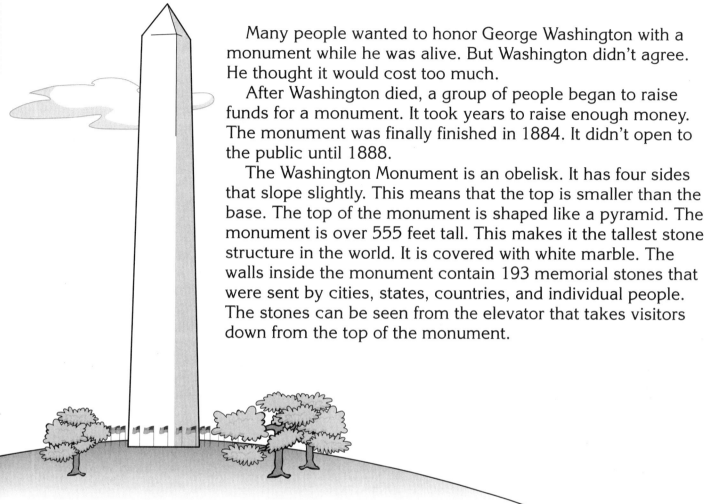

Many people wanted to honor George Washington with a monument while he was alive. But Washington didn't agree. He thought it would cost too much.

After Washington died, a group of people began to raise funds for a monument. It took years to raise enough money. The monument was finally finished in 1884. It didn't open to the public until 1888.

The Washington Monument is an obelisk. It has four sides that slope slightly. This means that the top is smaller than the base. The top of the monument is shaped like a pyramid. The monument is over 555 feet tall. This makes it the tallest stone structure in the world. It is covered with white marble. The walls inside the monument contain 193 memorial stones that were sent by cities, states, countries, and individual people. The stones can be seen from the elevator that takes visitors down from the top of the monument.

Draw a line to match each sentence starter to its ending.

1. Washington didn't want a monument built   an obelisk.

2. It took years to raise   in 1884.

3. Many groups sent   because it would be too expensive.

4. The Washington Monument is   money to build the monument.

5. The monument was finished   memorial stones.

Name _____

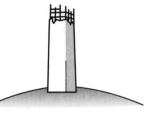

Remembering a President

Use the code to complete each fact.

1. George Washington is often called the __ __ __ __ __ __   __ __   __ __ __
                                               6 1 16 8 5 14   13 6   16 8 5

   __ __ __ __ __ __ __ .
    3 13 17 12 16 14 21

2. In 1833, people began to raise __ __ __ __ __ for a monument to honor Washington.
                                          6 17 12 4 15

3. Architect __ __ __ __ __ __   __ __ __ __ __ designed the monument.
                 14 13 2 5 14 16   11 9 10 10 15

4. It is made of marble and __ __ __ __ __ __ __ .
                           7 14 1 12 9 16 5

5. The walls at the base of the monument are __ __ __ __ __ __ __
                                         6 9 6 16 5 5 12

   feet thick.

6. The monument weighs over __ __ __ __ __ __ thousand tons.
                             12 9 12 5 16 21

7. The monument is __ __ __ __ __ __ on the inside.
                     8 13 10 10 13 19

8. To reach the top of the Washington Monument, visitors can ride an
   elevator or climb __ __ __ __ __   __ __ __ __ __ __ __
                         5 9 7 8 16   8 17 12 4 14 5 4

   __ __ __ __ __ __ - __ __ __ steps.
    12 9 12 5 16 21   15 9 20

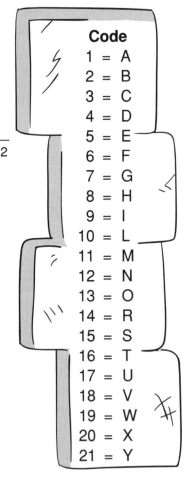

Code
1 = A
2 = B
3 = C
4 = D
5 = E
6 = F
7 = G
8 = H
9 = I
10 = L
11 = M
12 = N
13 = O
14 = R
15 = S
16 = T
17 = U
18 = V
19 = W
20 = X
21 = Y

Bonus Other monuments in Washington, DC, honor Abraham Lincoln, Thomas Jefferson, and Franklin D. Roosevelt. Choose one monument and find out what the monument looks like, who designed it, and how long it took to build.

Name _____

Lady Liberty

The Statue of Liberty was the first electric lighthouse.

In 1875, the French sculptor Frederic Auguste Bartholdi began building a statue. It was called *Liberty Enlightening the World.* Today it is known as the Statue of Liberty. Bartholdi designed the statue to be a lighthouse in Upper New York Bay. He planned to light her crown with lamps. U.S. leaders lit the torch with electricity instead.

Years after the statue arrived in America, they decided the statue did not make a good lighthouse. The torch was not bright enough. In 1902, the federal lighthouse board turned care of the statue over to the U.S. War Department. Then the National Park Service took over in 1933. More than 100 years later, millions of people still visit the statue each year.

Thickness of the copper skin: 2.4 millimeters

Height from toe to torch: 151' 1"

Weight: 225 tons

Complete each statement. Use the passage and illustration.

1. A _____ sculptor designed and built the Statue of Liberty.

2. The Statue of Liberty's full name is _____.

3. The sculptor wanted to light the statue's _____ to light the way for ships.

4. In 1902, the statue was no longer a _____.

5. The _____ takes care of the statue today.

6. _____ of people visit the Statue of Liberty each year.

7. The statue is about _____ feet tall and weighs_____ tons.

8. The statue's copper skin is only _____millimeters thick.

Lady Liberty

Decide whether each statement is a fact or an opinion.
Circle the letter in the matching column.

		Fact	Opinion
1.	Construction of the Statue of Liberty began in 1875.	E	A
2.	The statue is found in New York on Liberty Island.	M	N
3.	Most immigrants think the statue is a symbol of hope.	T	A
4.	France gave the Statue of Liberty to the United States as a gift.	L	R
5.	The statue's torch shines beautifully in the night sky.	Y	Z
6.	The Statue of Liberty was a working lighthouse for 16 years.	R	L
7.	The Statue of Liberty is a great lighthouse.	O	U
8.	*Liberty Enlightening the World* is the full name of the Statue of Liberty.	S	C

"Give me your tired, your poor,
Your huddled masses yearning
   to breathe free,
The wretched refuse of your
   teeming shore.
Send these, the homeless,
   tempest-tost to me,
I lift my lamp beside the golden
   door!"

Who wrote these famous words, found in the Statue of Liberty's museum?
To answer the question, match each answer above to a numbered line below.

___ ___ ___ ___   ___ ___ ___ ___ ___ ___ ___
 1   2   2   3   4   3   5   3   6   7   8

What do you think the boxed quote means? Explain.

©The Mailbox® • *Fascinating Facts: Social Studies* • TEC61067 • Key p. 126

Ringing Out Freedom

The Liberty Bell cracked the first time it was rung.

The Liberty Bell is a powerful symbol of American freedom. The bell was made in England for the 50th anniversary of the Pennsylvania colony. It arrived in Philadelphia in 1752 and was called the Old State House Bell. It cracked while being rung.

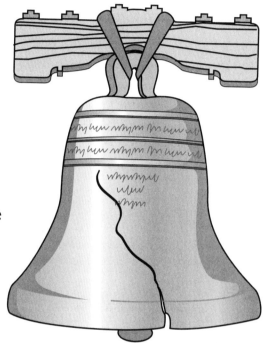

After being remade, it was used to call the Assembly together and to gather people for special events. On July 8, 1776, it called people to a public reading of the Declaration of Independence. Americans hid the bell during the Revolutionary War to keep it from being made into a cannon.

In 1835, the bell cracked again. A few years later, people who were against slavery started calling it the Liberty Bell. When it cracked again in 1846, people stopped ringing the bell. Now it is only tapped when marking special events. Thousands of people go to Philadelphia every year to see this great American symbol.

Answer each question with a complete sentence.

1. Why was the bell made? _____

   _____

2. Why was the bell rung on July 8, 1776? _____

   _____

3. Why was the bell hidden during the Revolutionary War? _____

   _____

4. Why did people start calling the Old State House Bell the Liberty Bell? _____

   _____

5. Why did people stop ringing the bell? _____

   _____

6. Why do people go to see the Liberty Bell? _____

   _____

Ringing Out Freedom

Read the clues.
Solve the puzzle.

Across
1. document read after ringing the bell on July 8, 1776
4. weight of the Liberty Bell is more than this
5. country where the Liberty Bell was first made
6. the last time the bell was rung was on this president's birthday in 1846
7. words inscribed on the Liberty Bell are from this book

Down
2. reason why the Liberty Bell had to be remade
3. colony that ordered the bell to be made
4. way that the Liberty Bell is rung now that its clapper has been removed

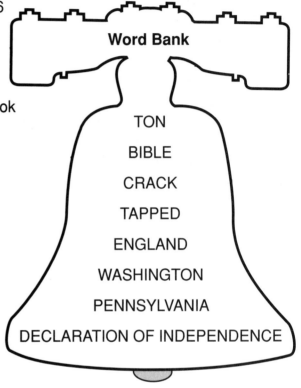

Word Bank

TON
BIBLE
CRACK
TAPPED
ENGLAND
WASHINGTON
PENNSYLVANIA
DECLARATION OF INDEPENDENCE

 The words inscribed on the bell are "Proclaim liberty throughout the land unto all the inhabitants thereof." Do you think they were a good choice? Why?

Name _____

A Presidential Path

The only U.S. president to be elected with no one voting against him was George Washington.

George Washington was the first president of the United States. Why did people feel that he was the right person to lead our country?

Up until then, Washington had worked hard on his family's plantation. There, he learned patience. He had surveyed land and explored the frontier. He had become a famous soldier and survived danger. His actions on the battlefield had earned him the respect and trust of his men. He had been in charge of the Continental Army when our country won its freedom from Great Britain.

After the war, Washington's officers would have made him king if he had let them. Instead, he helped our country become a place where the leader is chosen by the people. He was called the "Father of His Country."

Write "true" or "false."

_____ 1. George Washington led the colonists in the war against Great Britain.

_____ 2. Washington's work as a soldier did not help him become a good leader.

_____ 3. Washington wanted to become king of the United States.

_____ 4. Washington was admired and well liked.

_____ 5. When Washington was elected president, no one voted against him.

Name _____

A Presidential Path

Cut out each event card.
Read the event.
Then glue the card to the timeline.

| 1732 |
| 1749 |
| 1754 |
| 1755–58 |
| 1775 |
| 1781 |
| 1787 |
| 1789 |

George Washington was born in Virginia in 1732.

Washington was 43 years old when he became commander in chief of the Continental Army.

Five years after being hired as a land surveyor, he was a colonel in the French and Indian War.

Washington was 17 when he was hired to survey land in Virginia.

Six years after he became commander in chief, he won the battle that ended the Revolutionary War.

At age 57, George Washington became the first president of the United States.

He became president of the Constitutional Convention 55 years after he was born.

One year after being in the French and Indian War, he served three years as colonel of Virginia's frontier troops.

 Why do you think George Washington was a good leader? Explain.

74   ©The Mailbox® • Fascinating Facts: Social Studies • TEC61067 • Key p. 126

Name _____   **Thomas Jefferson**

Not Just a President

Thomas Jefferson sold his personal library to the Library of Congress.

Thomas Jefferson was a famous author and president. He is also known for designing buildings and his inventions. But did you know that he helped create our national library?

The Library of Congress was created in 1800. The books in the library were used by members of Congress. These books were kept inside the Capitol in Washington, DC. The British burned the Capitol during the War of 1812. All the books were ruined.

Thomas Jefferson had a library in his home. He offered the books to Congress. Congress paid him $23,950 for 6,487 books. Then a new library was created. Now the Library of Congress is the largest library in the world. It has over 130 million items. The library is open to all people, not just members of Congress.

Answer each question with a complete sentence.

1. For whom was the Library of Congress created? _____

_____

2. What happened to the first books in the library? _____

_____

3. How did Jefferson help the library? _____

_____

4. How has the library changed since 1800? _____

_____

Not Just a President

Read each sentence. Decide which category it belongs in.
Write the sentence number in the matching category.

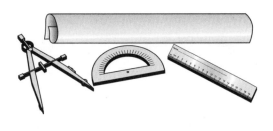

_____, _____, _____

ARCHITECT

_____, _____, _____

MUSICIAN

_____, _____, _____

SCIENTIST

_____, _____, _____

INVENTOR

1. Jefferson played the violin in chamber music concerts.

2. Jefferson grew and studied plants.

3. He designed the Virginia capitol.

4. Jefferson drew the plans for his home, Monticello.

5. He created a lap desk and a new type of plow.

6. Jefferson studied weather.

7. He practiced the violin two to three hours every day when he was young.

8. He played music with his wife.

9. Jefferson raised different kinds of sheep to see which ones had the best wool.

10. He invented a clock that showed the day and the time.

11. Jefferson created the decimal system we use to keep track of money.

12. He designed the first buildings at the University of Virginia.

Which word do you think best describes Thomas Jefferson: *president, writer, architect, musician, scientist,* **or** *inventor?* **Write a short paragraph on the back of this page explaining your answer.**

Man of Many Talents

Ben Franklin never made money from his inventions.

Ben Franklin lived in Philadelphia for many years. He did many things to make the city better. He started a public library. He also started a volunteer fire department. Ben saw that the city streets were dirty, dark, and unpaved. He worked hard to get the streets paved and lighted.

Ben liked to create things. He invented an electric battery, a lightning rod, and bifocal glasses. Bifocal glasses have lenses with two parts in the same frame. They allow people to see near and far. These glasses are still used today. Ben also designed the Franklin stove. It kept a room warmer than a fireplace. It helped people save money because it used less fuel. Many people used the stove to heat their homes.

Ben never used any of his ideas or designs for profit. He wanted all people to be able to use them to make their lives better.

Circle the letter of the best answer.

1. Benjamin Franklin lived in _____.
   a. Newport   b. Philadelphia   c. New York

2. Which of these did Ben **not** do to improve his city?
   a. start a volunteer fire department   b. start a library   c. build a playground

3. Ben invented a _____.
   a. lightning rod   b. electricity   c. magnifying glass

4. Which of these did the Franklin stove **not** do?
   a. light itself   b. use less fuel   c. heat a room better

5. Which of these would be a good title for this story?
   a. "A Generous Friend"   b. "The Franklin Stove"   c. "Helping Others"

Man of Many Talents

Ben Franklin was also a famous printer. He published *Poor Richard's Almanack.* This book was filled with advice, proverbs, weather predictions, jokes, and poems.

Use the code below to reveal some of Franklin's most famous proverbs.

Code

A	B	D	E	F	G	H	I	K	L	N	O	P	R	S	T	U	V	W	Y
1	2	3	4	5	6	7	8	9	10	11	12	13	14	15	16	17	18	19	20

1. __   __ __ __ __ __   __ __ __ __ __   __ __   __
    1   13 4 11 11 20   15 1 18 4 3   8 15   1

    __ __ __ __ __   __ __ __ __ __ __ .
    13 4 11 11 20   4 1 14 11 4 3

2. __ __ __ __ __ __   __ __ __ __   __ __ __ __
    2 4 16 16 4 14   15 10 8 13   19 8 16 7

    __ __ __ __   __ __ __ __   __ __ __ __ __ __ .
    5 12 12 16   16 7 1 11   16 12 11 6 17 4

3. __ __ __ __ __   __ __ __ __ __ __ __ ,   __ __ __ __ __ __
    6 14 4 1 16   16 1 10 9 4 14 15   10 8 16 16 10 4

    __ __ __ __ __ .
    3 12 4 14 15

4. ' __ __ __   __ __ __ __ __   __ __ __   __ __ __ ,   __ __ __ __
     16 8 15   4 1 15 20   16 12   15 4 4   7 1 14 3

    __ __   __ __ __ __ __ __ __ __ .
    16 12   5 12 14 4 15 4 4

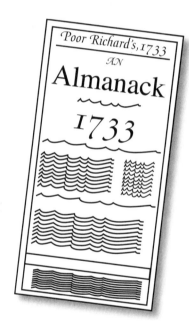

 Ben Franklin's proverbs show the qualities and traits that were important to him. Choose one and explain what you think it means.

MIDNIGHT RIDE

Paul Revere risked his own freedom to warn the patriots.

Would you take a risk to warn others of danger? Paul Revere did. He knew he could be arrested. Yet he wanted America to be free from the British.

When Paul found out British troops were moving, he had lanterns hung in a church steeple. They were a signal for the patriots in case he didn't complete his ride. Then he rode to Lexington. Paul warned the patriots there that the British were coming. Before he reached the next town, British soldiers caught Paul. They questioned him and let him go, but they took his horse.

After his ride, Paul carried more messages for the patriots. He became a soldier. He even printed paper money for the patriots. Each act was dangerous, but Paul had the courage to stand up for his beliefs.

Complete the sentences. Use the passage.

1. Paul could be _____ if he were caught.

2. Paul had _____ hung in a church steeple.

3. Paul rode to the town of _____.

4. He warned _____ that the British were on their way.

5. British soldiers took Paul's _____.

MIDNIGHT RIDE

Follow the directions below to draw Paul Revere's route on the map.

1. Color a blue dot at Boston. Paul started his journey here.

2. Color a blue dot at Charlestown. Paul traveled here by boat. Then he borrowed a horse and started to ride.

3. Draw a red *B* northwest of Charlestown, west of the river. British soldiers chased Paul here, but he got away.

4. Color a blue dot at Medford. Paul alerted the captain of the minutemen here.

5. Color a blue dot at Lexington. Here Paul told patriot leaders to leave to avoid capture.

6. Draw a blue dot and a red *B* about halfway between Lexington and Concord. Paul was caught here and questioned by the British.

7. Draw a dashed blue line to connect the dots on the map. Draw each symbol on the map key.

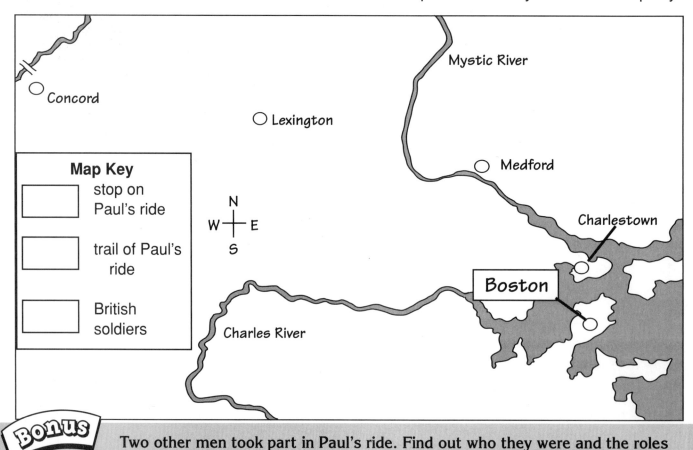

Bonus

Two other men took part in Paul's ride. Find out who they were and the roles they played in the famous ride.

©The Mailbox® • *Fascinating Facts: Social Studies* • TEC61067 • Key p. 126

Letter-Writing Lady

Abigail Adams and her husband were the first to live in the White House.

Do you like to write letters? Abigail Adams did! She is famous for the letters she wrote. Abigail was the wife of President John Adams. She wrote letters to him when he was away serving in the Continental Congress. The letters let us know what life in the colonies was like in the 1770s and 1780s. She also wrote him letters during the Revolutionary War. These letters gave her husband updates about the British troops and ships in the Boston area.

Abigail loved to read and was informed about many topics. She was concerned about women's rights. She also wanted girls to have more schooling. In a letter to her husband in 1776, she asked him to "remember the ladies" when making new laws.

In the fall of 1800, she and her family became the first to live in the White House. They lived there before the inside of the house was even complete!

**Unscramble the letters to form the missing words.
Write the words on the lines.**

1. Abigail was the ___ ___ ___ ___ of President John Adams. (fwie)

2. She is famous for her ___ ___ ___ ___ ___ ___ ___. (telerts)

3. Her letters tell us what life was like in the ___ ___ ___ ___ ___ ___ ___ ___. (noclsieo)

4. Her letters told her husband about what the ___ ___ ___ ___ ___ ___ ___ were doing in Boston. (stihirB)

5. Abigail Adams wanted more rights for ___ ___ ___ ___ ___. (ewmon)

Name _____

Abigail Adams

Letter-Writing Lady

Use the code to spell the missing word in each sentence.

1. Abigail Adams was born in ___ ___ ___ ___ ___ ___ ___ ___, Massachusetts, in 1744.
   4 22 2 14 12 6 7 19

2. She did not attend school much because of poor ___ ___ ___ ___ ___ ___.
   19 22 26 15 7 19

3. She read many books from her family's large ___ ___ ___ ___ ___ ___ ___.
   15 18 25 9 26 9 2

4. She married ___ ___ ___ ___ ___ ___ ___ ___ ___ on October 25, 1764.
   17 12 19 13   26 23 26 14 8

5. They had ___ ___ ___ ___ children.
   21 18 5 22

6. One of their sons, John Quincy, became the ___ ___ ___ ___ ___ president of the United States.
   8 18 3 7 19

7. Abigail ran the family farm when her husband was away serving in
   ___ ___ ___ ___ ___ ___ ___ ___.
   24 12 13 20 9 22 8 8

8. She wanted there to be more ___ ___ ___ ___ ___ ___ ___ ___ ___ for girls.
   8 24 19 12 12 15 18 13 20

9. Her letters during the ___ ___ ___ ___ ___ ___ ___ ___ ___ ___ ___ ___ ___ War told her
   9 22 5 12 15 6 7 18 12 13 26 9 2
   husband what the British were up to in the Boston area.

10. She was against ___ ___ ___ ___ ___ ___ ___.
    8 15 26 5 22 9 2

Code

A	B	C	D	E	F	G	H	I	J	K	L	M	N	O	P	Q	R	S	T	U	V	W	X	Y	Z
26	25	24	23	22	21	20	19	18	17	16	15	14	13	12	11	10	9	8	7	6	5	4	3	2	1

 Do you think letter writing is as important today as it was in Abigail's time? Why?

82

©The Mailbox® • Fascinating Facts: Social Studies • TEC61067 • Key p. 127

Hostess and Heroine

Dolley Madison saved a national treasure.

Dolley Madison was married to James Madison, the fourth president of the United States. Dolley was famous for the parties she hosted. Anyone could come; she sent no invitations. This often brought people with different views together. Dolley was very inviting and friendly. This made others feel more comfortable around one another.

During this time, America was at war with Britain. In 1814, Dolley was at the White House when the British attacked Washington, DC. Most everyone fled. Even the soldiers who were supposed to be protecting the house left. Dolley stayed behind to pack important papers and pieces of silver. She also made sure that a famous painting of George Washington was sent to safety. Then she left the house. British soldiers burned the president's home a few hours later. But Dolley had rescued a national treasure. The George Washington portrait she saved still hangs in the White House today.

Make each sentence true. Cross out the word that does not belong. Write a word from the word bank above it. Not all words will be used.

1. Dolley was married to the 14th president.

2. Dolley's guests always felt worried.

3. The British painted the White House during the War of 1812.

4. The first lady donated a famous portrait of George Washington.

Word Bank
poem
welcome
saved
sixth
capitol
burned
fourth

Hostess and Heroine

If the statement is a fact, color the frame green.
If the statement is an opinion, color the frame purple.

1. Dolley Madison gave the best parties.

2. Her husband was a president of the United States.

3. Dolley saved a famous painting of George Washington.

4. Dolley should have been scared when she heard that the British troops were coming.

5. Dolley probably should have saved other items too.

6. The same portrait of George Washington hangs in the White House today.

7. British troops burned the White House in 1814.

8. Dolley was brave to save an important national symbol.

Bonus

Explain why you think Dolley Madison hosted so many parties at the White House.

©The Mailbox® • *Fascinating Facts: Social Studies* • TEC61067 • Key p. 127

Name _____

The Mother of Black Literature

Phillis Wheatley's book of poetry was the first book published by an African American.

In 1761, a young African girl arrived in Boston on a slave ship. John Wheatley bought her to do chores for his wife. They named her Phillis after the ship that brought her to the colonies. The Wheatleys began teaching Phillis to read and write. In fact, she was treated more like a family member than a slave. Phillis was an eager student.

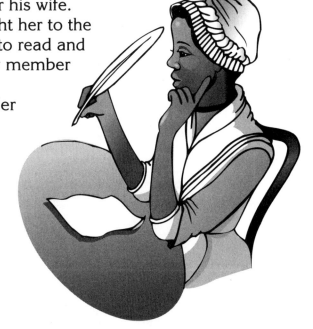

As a teenager, Phillis began to write poetry. Her first poem was published in a newspaper. She was about 14 years old! Six years later, Phillis traveled to England. Her book of poetry was published there. Also, George Washington praised Phillis for a poem written in his honor. She was even invited to meet the new general!

Phillis's poetry still inspires people today. She achieved much at a time when most African Americans were still slaves.

Answer each question with a complete sentence.

1. Why was Phillis Wheatley brought to Boston? _____

   _____

2. What fact supports the statement that Phillis was treated like a family member? _____

   _____

3. Where was Phillis's first poem published? _____

   _____

4. Why did George Washington invite Phillis to come and meet him? _____

   _____

The Mother of Black Literature

Write a letter in the blank for each ordered pair.
If your answers are correct, you will spell the words that complete each sentence.

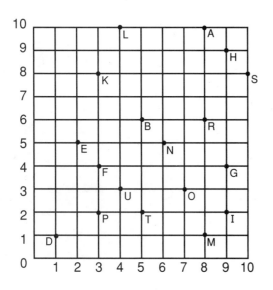

1. Phillis was ___ ___ ___ ___ ___ ___ ___ ___ ___ from Africa. She came to
   (3, 8) (9, 2) (1, 1) (6, 5) (8, 10) (3, 2) (3, 2) (2, 5) (1, 1)

   ___ ___ ___ ___ ___ ___ on a slave ship named *The* ___ ___ ___ ___ ___ ___ ___.
   (5, 6) (7, 3) (10, 8) (5, 2) (7, 3) (6, 5)   (3, 2) (9, 9) (9, 2) (4, 10) (4, 10) (9, 2) (10, 8)

2. Phillis learned much from the Wheatleys. She began writing ___ ___ ___ ___ ___ ___ ___ like
   (4, 10) (2, 5) (5, 2) (5, 2) (2, 5) (8, 6) (10, 8)

   her mistress. Then Phillis started writing poetry. She wrote many ___ ___ ___ ___ ___ ___ ___,
   (2, 5) (4, 10) (2, 5) (9, 4) (9, 2) (2, 5) (10, 8)

   or poems written for a person who had ___ ___ ___ ___. Many of these poems honored well-
   (1, 1) (9, 2) (2, 5) (1, 1)

   known ___ ___ ___ ___ ___ ___ ___. Some were printed in newspapers.
   (4, 10) (2, 5) (8, 10) (1, 1) (2, 5) (8, 6) (10, 8)

3. While on her trip to ___ ___ ___ ___ ___ ___ ___, Phillis met Ben ___ ___ ___ ___ ___ ___ ___ ___.
   (2, 5) (6, 5) (9, 4) (4, 10) (8, 10) (6, 5) (1, 1)   (3, 4) (8, 6) (8, 10) (6, 5) (3, 8) (4, 10) (9, 2) (6, 5)

   She was supposed to meet with ___ ___ ___ ___ ___ ___ ___ ___ ___ ___, too. But her
   (3, 8) (9, 2) (6, 5) (9, 4) (9, 4) (2, 5) (7, 3) (8, 6) (9, 4) (2, 5)

   visit to London was shortened. Phillis had to return to Boston to care for Mrs. Wheatley, who

   had become ___ ___ ___.
   (9, 2) (4, 10) (4, 10)

4. After getting her ___ ___ ___ ___ ___ ___ ___, Phillis ___ ___ ___ ___ ___ ___ ___ John
   (3, 4) (8, 6) (2, 5) (2, 5) (1, 1) (7, 3) (8, 1)   (8, 1) (8, 10) (8, 6) (8, 6) (9, 2) (2, 5) (1, 1)

   Peters, a free black man. But their married life was ___ ___ ___ ___ ___. She died at about
   (10, 8) (9, 9) (7, 3) (8, 6) (5, 2)

   the age of 30.

 **Bonus**

How do you think Phillis Wheatley could have made a difference in the lives of
African Americans and women if she had lived longer? Explain.

Fight for Truth

Sojourner Truth spoke both Dutch and English but could not read or write.

Sojourner Truth's birth name was Isabella Baumfree. She was born a slave in New York. After many years of slavery, she was freed under a New York antislavery law in 1828. She later changed her name to Sojourner. She spent much of her time giving speeches. Sojourner was the first black woman to speak out publicly against slavery. People loved her strong voice and words when she spoke. During the Civil War, she raised money for black soldiers serving in the army by singing and preaching.

She once visited the White House and met President Abraham Lincoln. After that, she stayed in Washington, DC. While there, she helped slaves who had escaped from the south find jobs. She also attempted to convince the federal government to give blacks land in the West. Despite her inability to read or write, she had a great impact on the lives of people in the 1800s.

Complete each sentence. Use the passage.

1. Sojourner Truth was first called _____ .

2. Sojourner spoke out against _____ .

3. When she spoke, people loved her strong _____ and _____ .

4. Sojourner spoke both _____ and _____ .

5. She helped raise _____ for black troops fighting in the Civil War.

Fight For Truth

Unscramble the letters to form the missing word. Then match each definition to the correct term.

A. a person who wanted to __ __ slavery (dne)

B. a person who helps others gain __ __ __ __ __ rights (uqela)

C. a person who tries to __ __ __ __ __ (peaces)

D. a person forced to __ __ __ __ as the property of another (rokw)

E. Sojourner Truth's birth __ __ __ __ (mena)

F. a place to __ __ __ and sell slaves (uyb)

G. a conflict between citizens of the __ __ __ __ country (mesa)

H. the practice of __ __ __ __ __ __ people and forcing them to work (nwonig)

___ 1. equal rights advocate

___ 2. slavery

___ 3. auction

___ 4. abolitionist

___ 5. fugitive

___ 6. Isabella

___ 7. civil war

___ 8. slave

Bonus Research Sojourner Truth's life and create a timeline.

©The Mailbox® • Fascinating Facts: Social Studies • TEC61067 • Key p. 127

FREEDOM'S GUIDE

Harriet Tubman received a silver medal from the queen of England.

Harriet Tubman was well known for her work with the Underground Railroad. But first, she had to travel it to escape her own slavery. She was born a slave. As a young adult, Harriet vowed to reach freedom. Even her husband doubted that she could run away safely. But Harriet made it! The secret paths and the helpful people along the way moved her toward freedom! Then she helped other slaves flee. During the 1850s, Harriet helped about 300 slaves escape. She became a famous abolitionist!

During the Civil War, she aided the Union army. She kept helping freed slaves after the war. She raised money for black schools.

In 1913, Harriet Tubman was buried with military honors. At last, her service during the Civil War was honored. Later, a World War II ship was named for her. Her portrait was put on a U.S. stamp. Harriet Tubman's honors are many!

Circle the best answer for each sentence.

1. Harriet Tubman began life as a (slave, abolitionist).

2. The Underground Railroad was a system of (trains, secret paths) that helped slaves reach freedom.

3. An abolitionist is against (freedom, slavery).

4. Harriet Tubman was buried with military honors because of her service to the (Underground Railroad, Union army).

5. Around the world, Harriet's actions were (honored, condemned).

Name _____

FREEDOM'S GUIDE

Unscramble the letters to form the missing words.
Then circle each word in the puzzle.

1. As a child, Harriet changed her name so she would have the same name as her

   _____. (rtomeh)

2. As a teenager, Harriet's master hit her in the head with a _____. (krco) She was trying to protect another slave.

3. The Underground Railroad helped slaves escape. They went to the northern United States or to _____. (dnCaaa)

4. Harriet helped many members of her _____ escape to freedom. (mlyafi)

5. At one time, there was a $40,000 _____ for Harriet's capture. (wraedr)

6. During the Civil War, Harriet was a _____ for the Union army. (yps)

D	R	L	B	G	S	F	N	E	I
P	R	V	O	U	T	R	O	C	K
R	E	H	T	O	M	Y	W	J	C
J	W	E	G	C	A	R	Y	P	M
U	A	M	S	A	K	L	M	N	C
B	R	E	I	O	I	T	G	Y	A
T	D	W	V	M	Z	D	U	I	N
H	X	O	A	R	Q	S	K	S	A
A	I	F	Q	F	Y	P	S	H	D
M	P	R	O	T	E	C	T	L	A

 After the Civil War, Harriet went to South Carolina. There she set up schools for the newly freed slaves. Do you think she was fearful of living in a southern state? Explain.

©The Mailbox® • Fascinating Facts: Social Studies • TEC61067 • Key p. 127

FREEDOM FIGHTER

About 70 years before Rosa Parks was born, Frederick Douglass refused to give up his seat on trains.

Frederick Augustus Washington Bailey was a slave for almost 20 years. Then he escaped to the North. Once there, he changed his name to Frederick Douglass. Douglass then spent his life fighting and speaking for African Americans' and women's rights.

In the early 1840s, Douglass fought segregation. He would sit in "Whites Only" train cars until he was dragged away. He also published an antislavery newspaper called *The North Star*. In his spare time, he allowed other runaway slaves to use his house as a stop on the Underground Railroad.

When the Civil War broke out, Douglass helped recruit African Americans for the Union army. He also met three times with President Lincoln to discuss how to end slavery and win the war.

Douglass went on to become the first African American to hold a high rank in the U.S. government. He was also one of the most famous African American men of the 19th century.

Write "true" or "false."

_____ 1. Frederick Douglass was a runaway slave.

_____ 2. Douglass's real name was Bailey Washington.

_____ 3. Douglass would not sit in "Whites Only" train cars.

_____ 4. Frederick Douglass's house was a stop on the Underground Railroad.

_____ 5. Douglass helped recruit for the Rebel army in the Civil War.

_____ 6. President Lincoln and Frederick Douglass met many times.

_____ 7. Douglass wanted to end slavery.

_____ 8. Frederick Douglass was one of the most famous African American men of the 20th century.

FREEDOM FIGHTER

Unscramble the letters to form each missing word. Write your answer in the puzzle.

1. *The North Star* newspaper was named for slaves following the North Star in the sky to _____. (OEEDMRF)

2. Douglass wanted _____ to have equal rights. (OIEIISNMTR)

3. Frederick Douglass died on _____ 20, 1895. (RAYBEFRU)

4. *My Bondage and My Freedom* is one version of Douglass's _____. (OTUAIOBPHGARY)

5. Douglass wanted President _____ to free all slaves. (LLNOCIN)

6. Frederick Douglass was a _____ for almost 20 years. (VALES)

7. Douglass created a _____ called *The North Star*. (SPANWERPE)

8. The Equal Rights Party asked Douglass to run for vice _____ of the United States. (DERPSITEN)

Crossword column: D O U G L A S S

"I appear this evening as a thief and a robber. I stole this head, these limbs, this body from my master, and ran off with them."
Frederick Douglass, circa 1842

 Explain what you think was meant by the quote above.

The Plant Doctor

George Washington Carver made more than 300 products from peanuts.

George Washington Carver loved plants. He fell in love with them on the farm where he was born near the end of the Civil War. George, a slave, was a sickly child and could not work in the fields. So he cared for the garden plants, which thrived. His success with nursing sick plants back to health earned him the nickname the Plant Doctor.

George was about 11 when he started school. He went on to college and studied agriculture. He wanted to help people who worked on farms. George used his knowledge to teach farmers a system of crop rotation. He also did research. He is most famous for his research on peanuts. But he also made products from pecans, sweet potatoes, and other plants. He could have become rich, but he chose to use his talents to help others instead.

Unscramble the letters to form the missing word.

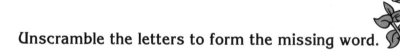

1. George Washington Carver was not a __ __ __ __ __ __ child. (gotnrs)

2. He worked in the __ __ __ __ __ __ because he could not work in the fields. (dregan)

3. He was called the Plant Doctor because he could __ __ __ __ __ sick plants back to health. (runes)

4. He chose to study __ __ __ __ __ __ __ __ __ __ __ in college. (giucarurlet)

5. He taught farmers how to __ __ __ __ __ __ their crops to help the soil. (torate)

6. He became famous for his __ __ __ __ __ __ __ __ on peanuts. (hacreser)

Name _____

The Plant Doctor

Cut out the cards.
Glue each card below its matching effect.

1. As a boy, George cared for garden plants instead of working in the fields.

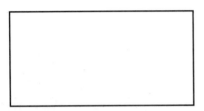

2. He was given the nickname the Plant Doctor.

3. George taught farmers how to rotate planting peanuts, pecans, and other crops to enrich the soil.

4. He studied agriculture in college.

5. He came up with over 300 products made from peanuts.

6. He is famous for more than his research on peanuts.

 **Bonus** In 1940, George Washington Carver gave away his savings of $33,000 for research. Why do you think he did this?

©The Mailbox® • *Fascinating Facts: Social Studies* • TEC61067 • Key p. 128

George also created products from sweet potatoes and pecans.

He could nurse sick plants back to health.

George wanted to help farmers.

He was a sickly child and not very strong.

He did a lot of research on peanuts.

Growing only cotton depleted, or wore out, the soil.

Name _____

Hustle and Bustle

About one out of every six Americans lives in the megalopolis of the Northeast!

A megalopolis is a group of cities that have expanded and grown together. They grow until they almost form one massive city. The Northeast holds the largest megalopolis in the United States. It stretches for about 600 miles! The area from Boston to New York to Washington, DC, is a megalopolis some people call Boswash.

Getting around in many large cities can be complex. Instead of driving, many people use public transportation. Buses and subways transport scores of people every day. Light-rail vehicles, such as trolleys, also move the public around the region.

Factories in the Northeast produce goods for the world. A host of rivers are used to move the cargo to port cities along the coast. The deep harbors in the region make it a center for global trade. This megalopolis is a busy place that keeps changing and growing.

Make each sentence true. Cross out the word that does not belong. Write a word from the word bank above it. Not all words will be used.

1. The area from Boston to Washington, DC, is a metropolis.

2. People use more private transportation in a large city.

3. Few people live in the northeastern megalopolis.

4. The midwestern megalopolis stretches for about 600 miles.

5. The shallow ports make the Northeast a good place for worldwide trade.

Word Bank
megalopolis
poor
deep
northeastern
fast
many
public
meters

Hustle and Bustle

Cut out the boxes below.
Glue each box under the correct category.

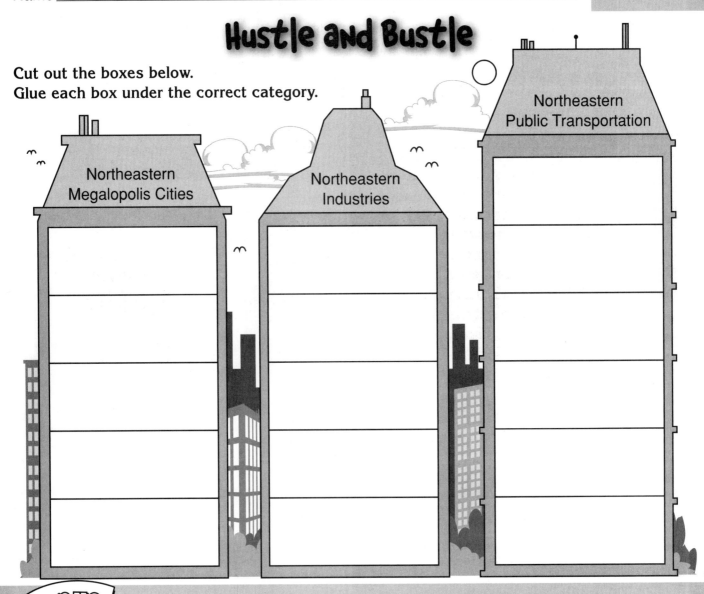

Northeastern Megalopolis Cities

Northeastern Industries

Northeastern Public Transportation

Bonus Do you think more goods are sent worldwide by airplane or by ship? Explain.

©The Mailbox® • Fascinating Facts: Social Studies • TEC61067 • Key p. 128

boats	finance	Baltimore	trolleys
taxis	communications	New York City	buses
tourism	Boston	medical research	Washington, DC
subways	Philadelphia	factories	airplanes

Name _____

MOVING ON

NASCAR racing originated in the Southeast.

Tourism brings many people to the southeastern United States. Some come for the splendid mountains. Others enjoy the theme parks. The winters are very mild in this region. Many people come to visit the sandy beaches during this time of year. But fans of stock car racing are lured by NASCAR races.

NASCAR is an acronym that stands for National Association for Stock Car Auto Racing. Stock car racing is the most popular type of car racing in the United States. The Southeast is known as the birthplace of stock car racing. The first NASCAR race took place in Charlotte, North Carolina. Many important races remain there today. The Daytona 500 is held in Daytona Beach, Florida. The Talladega 500 is run in Talladega, Alabama. And the Southern 500 is held in Darlington, South Carolina. Wherever the races are held, many people will be there, which helps the tourism industry of the Southeast.

Circle the letter of the best answer.

1. Many people visit the southeastern region because of its _____.
   a. coastal areas
   b. NASCAR races
   c. both a and b

2. NASCAR stands for _____.
   a. National Association of Southern Cars and Racers
   b. National Association for South Carolina and Its Region
   c. National Association for Stock Car Auto Racing

3. The first NASCAR race was held in _____.
   a. Talladega, Alabama
   b. Charlotte, North Carolina
   c. Darlington, South Carolina

4. The Southeast is seen as the birthplace of _____.
   a. mountain lodges
   b. theme parks
   c. stock car racing

98 Name _____

MOVING ON

Use the code to find the names of some tourist spots in the southeastern United States.

Code

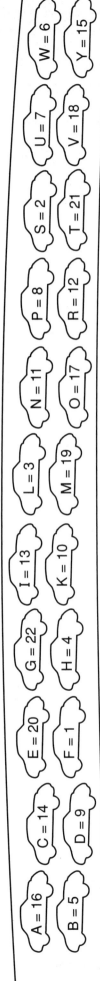

A = 16   C = 14   E = 20   G = 22   I = 13   K = 10
B = 5   D = 9   F = 1   H = 4   L = 3   N = 11   P = 8   S = 2   U = 7   W = 6
                                    M = 19   O = 17   R = 12   T = 21   V = 18   Y = 15

1. The largest rock dome in North America is in Georgia. A sculpture of Civil War leaders is carved into the rock.

   $\overline{2}$ $\overline{21}$ $\overline{17}$ $\overline{11}$ $\overline{20}$ $\overline{19}$ $\overline{17}$ $\overline{7}$ $\overline{11}$ $\overline{21}$ $\overline{16}$ $\overline{13}$ $\overline{11}$

2. This city in Virginia has been restored to look much like it did in colonial times.

   $\overline{6}$ $\overline{13}$ $\overline{3}$ $\overline{3}$ $\overline{16}$ $\overline{19}$ $\overline{2}$ $\overline{5}$ $\overline{7}$ $\overline{12}$ $\overline{22}$

3. This site is Kentucky's most famous natural wonder.

   $\overline{19}$ $\overline{16}$ $\overline{19}$ $\overline{19}$ $\overline{17}$ $\overline{21}$ $\overline{4}$ $\overline{14}$ $\overline{16}$ $\overline{18}$ $\overline{20}$

4. Maryland boasts this site where the U.S. national anthem was written.

   $\overline{1}$ $\overline{17}$ $\overline{12}$ $\overline{21}$ $\overline{19}$ $\overline{14}$ $\overline{4}$ $\overline{20}$ $\overline{11}$ $\overline{12}$ $\overline{15}$

5. Huntsville, Alabama, holds the world's largest group of space-related objects.

   $\overline{7}$ $\overline{2}$. $\overline{2}$ $\overline{8}$ $\overline{16}$ $\overline{14}$ $\overline{20}$ and $\overline{12}$ $\overline{17}$ $\overline{14}$ $\overline{10}$ $\overline{20}$ $\overline{21}$

   $\overline{14}$ $\overline{20}$ $\overline{11}$ $\overline{21}$ $\overline{20}$ $\overline{12}$

6. A racetrack in this North Carolina city held the first NASCAR race.

   $\overline{14}$ $\overline{4}$ $\overline{16}$ $\overline{12}$ $\overline{3}$ $\overline{17}$ $\overline{21}$ $\overline{21}$ $\overline{20}$

7. This group of islands stretches into the Gulf of Mexico. Superb coral reefs are found here.

   $\overline{1}$ $\overline{3}$ $\overline{17}$ $\overline{12}$ $\overline{13}$ $\overline{9}$ $\overline{16}$ $\overline{10}$ $\overline{20}$ $\overline{20}$ $\overline{15}$ $\overline{2}$

8. This park in Arkansas is built around hot waters. People claim that the waters relieve pain.

   $\overline{4}$ $\overline{17}$ $\overline{21}$ $\overline{2}$ $\overline{8}$ $\overline{12}$ $\overline{13}$ $\overline{11}$ $\overline{22}$ $\overline{2}$ $\overline{11}$ $\overline{16}$ $\overline{21}$ $\overline{13}$ $\overline{17}$ $\overline{11}$ $\overline{16}$ $\overline{3}$

   $\overline{8}$ $\overline{16}$ $\overline{12}$ $\overline{10}$

BONUS Why do you think tourism is important to the southeastern United States? Explain.

FEEL THE HEAT

Some of the hottest temperatures in the United States are in the Southwest.

Arizona, New Mexico, Texas, and Oklahoma have all recorded record-breaking temperatures of 120°F and above. These states are known for their hot weather. New Mexico, Arizona, and western Texas have a dry climate. Cacti are not an uncommon sight. East Texas and Oklahoma are cooler.

These states are not entirely hot and desertlike. In the winter these states have also recorded subzero temperatures. Both New Mexico and Arizona have reached temperatures of –40°F or below. Texas and Oklahoma have been as low as –23°F. It is not unusual for the northern areas of the states to receive up to 30 inches of snow annually. The mountains in New Mexico have even been known to receive as much as 300 inches of snow in one year! Thousands of skiers flock to resorts in the mountains each ski season.

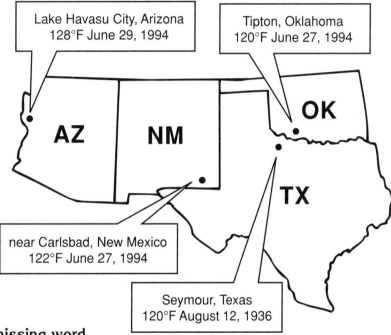

Record-Breaking Temperatures

Lake Havasu City, Arizona
128°F June 29, 1994

Tipton, Oklahoma
120°F June 27, 1994

near Carlsbad, New Mexico
122°F June 27, 1994

Seymour, Texas
120°F August 12, 1936

Unscramble the letters to form the missing word.

1. The southwest has some of the _____ temperatures in the United States. (stehtot)

2. New Mexico and Arizona have dry _____. (micltaes)

3. East Texas and Oklahoma have _____ temperatures. (loorec)

4. The hottest temperature ever recorded in Arizona was in Lake _____. (saaHvu ytiC)

5. The _____ between the hottest temperature in Texas and the hottest temperature in New Mexico is 2°F. (deenecfrfi)

FEEL THE HEAT

Use the clues to answer each question.

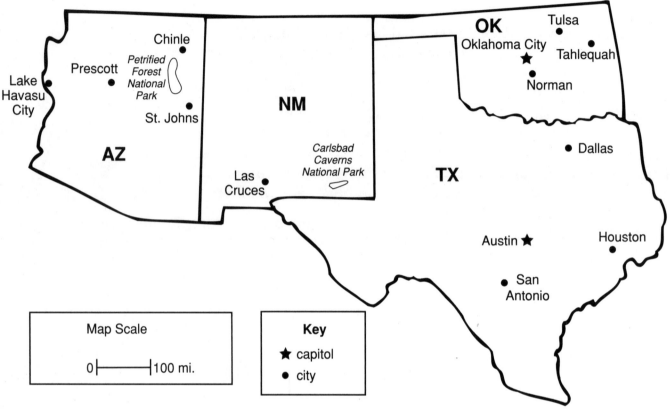

1. What city in Arizona had a record-breaking temperature of 128°F on June 29, 1994? (about 125 miles west of Prescott, Arizona) _____

2. Which state has had almost 300 inches of snow in one year? (west of Texas and east of Arizona) _____

3. In which city in Oklahoma is the Cherokee Heritage Center? (about 60 miles southeast of Tulsa, Oklahoma) _____

4. In what national park can you find trees that have turned to stone? (south of Chinle, Arizona, and north of St. Johns, Arizona) _____

5. In what city is the Alamo, an old Spanish mission? (about 80 miles southwest of Austin, Texas)

_____

6. What national park has hundreds of thousands of bats that fly at dusk? (about 140 miles east of Las Cruces, New Mexico) _____

7. Where might you go in Oklahoma to see the Rodeo Hall of Fame? (about 20 miles north of Norman, Oklahoma) _____

8. Where is NASA's headquarters located? (about 200 miles southeast of Dallas, Texas)

_____

THE NATION'S BREADBASKET

There are more foods made with wheat than any other cereal grain.

In the midwestern region of the United States, there are miles of flat land. Rich soil makes this land perfect for farms. Farmers grow grains, fruits, and vegetables. These crops provide us with many items that we eat each day. A lot of cereal is made in Battle Creek, Michigan. So much is produced that it is called the Cereal Bowl of America.

Some of the crops are grown for other reasons. They are also used to feed farm animals. The region raises lots of animals for food. There are many hog, beef cattle, and chicken farms. They provide the nation with meat products. Meat-packing plants process the livestock. Then the meat is sent to supermarkets. Dairy farms of the Midwest are known for the milk, butter, and cheese that they produce. Wisconsin holds the title of America's Dairyland.

The Midwest covers the tables of the nation with tasty and healthy food.

Complete each sentence. Use the passage.

1. The rich soil found on the flat midwestern land is good for _____ crops.

2. Farmers grow crops to feed _____ and _____.

3. Battle Creek, Michigan, is known for its production of _____.

4. _____ churns out many milk products.

5. The Midwest is called the nation's breadbasket because _____

_____.

Name _____

THE NATION'S BREADBASKET

Write a word from the word bank to complete each sentence.

1. John __ __ __ __ __ invented the first steel plow.
   　9

   It helped midwestern farmers turn the prairie soil.

2. __ __ __ __ can drink a bathtub full of water a day!
   　10

3. Iowa farmers raise more than 25 million __ __ __ __
   　　　　　　　　　　　　　　　　　　　　12
   a year!

4. Kansas's leading crop is __ __ __ __ __.
   　　　　　　　　　　　　　 1

Word Bank

cities	people
hogs	Deere
Ohio	soybeans
cows	McCormick
wheat	irrigation

5. An acre of __ __ __ __ __ __ __ __ can be used to produce more than 80,000 crayons.
   　　　　　　　　　 3　4

6. Each U.S. farmer produces enough food to feed 78 __ __ __ __ __ __.
   　　　　　　　　　　　　　　　　　　　　　　　　　11

7. Cyrus __ __ __ __ __ __ __ __ __ invented a reaping machine. Grain no longer had to
   　　　7　　　　　　　　　5
   be cut by hand.

8. Dairy farms need to be near __ __ __ __ __ __. Milk can reach shoppers while it is still
   　　　　　　　　　　　　　　　8　　　　6
   fresh.

9. __ __ __ __ farmers have grown apples since the days of Johnny Appleseed.
   　2

10. __ __ __ __ __ __ __ __ __ __ is used on many farms in South Dakota to water the
    　　　　　　　　　 13
    crops.

What should you say after eating your breakfast?
To answer the question, match the letters above to the numbered lines below.

__ __ __ __ __ __, __ __ __ __ __ __ __!
1　2　3　4　5　6　　7　8　9　10　11　12　13

 **What do you think would help midwestern farmers produce even better crops? Explain.**

©The Mailbox® • *Fascinating Facts: Social Studies* • TEC61067 • Key p. 128

VALUABLE RESOURCES

Giant sequoias are the largest living things on the earth!

On the Pacific Coast, the forests are one of the region's most priceless natural resources. Oregon, California, and Washington are the nation's top lumber states. The trees are vital for many reasons. Timber production brings money into the region. Some endangered species live around the trees. If the old forests are cut, the species might become extinct. Also, the trees' roots help preserve the water supply. The roots soak up rain and prevent runoff.

Some of the earth's largest and oldest living things are the trees of California. Redwoods are the tallest living things in the world. One measures almost 370 feet tall! The fastest growing tree is the giant sequoia. At up to 300 feet tall, their trunks can measure 100 feet around! Bristlecone pines are the oldest living things. Some have lived more than 4,000 years! It is easy to see why trees are so important in the West.

Answer each question with a complete sentence.

1. Why is timber production important in the West?

   _____

   _____

2. What might be an effect of cutting down old trees?

   _____

   _____

3. How do trees help preserve water? _____

   _____

4. How big can giant sequoias grow? _____

   _____

Name _____

VALUABLE RESOURCES

Decide whether each sentence is a fact or an opinion.
Write the number on the correct tree.

1. One important natural resource on the Pacific Coast is fish.

2. Finding oil in the West would be exciting.

3. Large reserves of coal and petroleum are found in Montana.

4. In Colorado, water is valued because it is scarce in some areas.

5. The coastal inlets and bays provide the best fishing in the country.

6. Idaho has many types of soil.

7. Natural gas is found in Oregon and Utah.

8. The West would be a good place to live.

9. The forests of Wyoming create the best places for parks.

10. Gold is a metal that prompted a gold rush in California.

Opinions

Facts

Bonus

How can the natural resources of the West help the economy? Explain.

©The Mailbox® • Fascinating Facts: Social Studies • TEC61067 • Key p. 128

The Fascinating Facts About Social Studies Game

Getting Ready to Play

1. Make a copy of the game cards on pages 106–120. Laminate the cards for durability.
2. Divide students into teams of two to four players each.
3. Sort the cards into three stacks: true/false, multiple choice, and fill in the blank.
4. Explain the point system to students:
    true/false = 5 points
    multiple choice = 10 points
    fill in the blank = 15 points

How to Play

1. Player 1 on Team 1 chooses the type of question he wants to answer: true/false, multiple choice, or fill in the blank.
2. The teacher reads aloud the question on the top card of the appropriate stack. If the player answers correctly, his team receives the appropriate number of points.
3. If that player answers incorrectly, Player 1 on Team 2 gets an opportunity to answer the question correctly and earn points for his team. (If the question was a true/false question, the opponent will automatically get it correct if he was listening.) If he answers incorrectly, no team earns the points and the teacher gives the correct answer.
4. The game continues with a player from Team 3 choosing the type of question he wants to answer.
5. The first team to earn 50 points wins. To extend the game, play until one team earns 100 points.

Variation

Use the game cards as flash cards with the whole class. Shuffle all of the cards into one stack and ask one question at a time from the top of the deck. Award one point for each correct answer. Use the game to review just the topic(s) you've recently covered or use all the cards as a fun year-end review.

Game Cards

EXPLORERS & EXPLORATIONS

True or False:

Christopher Columbus used no instruments to guide him across the Atlantic Ocean.

(False)

TEC61067

EXPLORERS & EXPLORATIONS

Juan Ponce de León died from a wound received while trying to colonize (<u>Florida</u>).

TEC61067

EXPLORERS & EXPLORATIONS

Christopher Columbus's discovery _____.

(a) opened a new route to Asia
(b) helped Spain find gold
(c) exposed people on two continents to each other and to new diseases, plants, and animals

TEC61067

EXPLORERS & EXPLORATIONS

True or False:

Francisco Vasquez de Coronado found the Seven Cities of Cibola.

(False)

TEC61067

EXPLORERS & EXPLORATIONS

Christopher Columbus was looking for a sea route to (<u>Asia</u>).

TEC61067

EXPLORERS & EXPLORATIONS

Francisco Vasquez de Coronado explored the _____.

(a) southwestern United States
(b) southeastern United States
(c) Mexico

TEC61067

EXPLORERS & EXPLORATIONS

True or False:

Juan Ponce de León was a French explorer.

(False)

TEC61067

EXPLORERS & EXPLORATIONS

Years after (<u>Francisco Vasquez de Coronado's</u>) exploration, silver and copper would be found underground in the American Southwest.

TEC61067

EXPLORERS & EXPLORATIONS

Juan Ponce de León conquered the island of _____.

(a) Puerto Rico
(b) Cuba
(c) Hispaniola

TEC61067

EXPLORERS & EXPLORATIONS

True or False:

Robert La Salle explored the Missouri River.

(False)

TEC61067

©The Mailbox® • *Fascinating Facts: Social Studies* • TEC61067

EXPLORERS & EXPLORATIONS

Robert La Salle hoped to become wealthier by _____.

(a) finding gold
(b) trading land
(c) trading fur

TEC61067

EXPLORERS & EXPLORATIONS

True or False:

Henry Hudson sailed for the English and the Dutch.

(True)

TEC61067

EXPLORERS & EXPLORATIONS

Robert La Salle claimed the land around the Mississippi River and its tributaries for (France).

TEC61067

EXPLORERS & EXPLORATIONS

Henry Hudson sailed _____.

(a) to China
(b) farther north than any explorer before him
(c) to the Pacific Ocean

TEC61067

EXPLORERS & EXPLORATIONS

True or False:

Samuel de Champlain went to Canada searching for a route to Asia.

(True)

TEC61067

EXPLORERS & EXPLORATIONS

Henry Hudson was looking for a sea route to (Asia).

TEC61067

EXPLORERS & EXPLORATIONS

Samuel de Champlain's explorations _____.
(a) helped France colonize New France
(b) led to the discovery of Lake Champlain
(c) both a and b

TEC61067

EXPLORERS & EXPLORATIONS

True or False:

John Smith helped make Jamestown a successful colony.

(True)

TEC61067

EXPLORERS & EXPLORATIONS

Samuel de Champlain founded the city of (Quebec).

TEC61067

EXPLORERS & EXPLORATIONS

John Smith traded with local tribes for _____.

(a) food
(b) land
(c) gold

TEC61067

Game Cards

EXPLORERS & EXPLORATIONS	John Smith wouldn't let the Jamestown colonists eat if they didn't (work).	REVOLUTIONARY WAR	The colonists threw over _____ chests of tea into Boston Harbor. (a) 300 (b) 30 (c) 3,000

TEC61067   TEC61067

REVOLUTIONARY WAR	**True or False:** The American colonists did not want to be taxed without having representation in Parliament. **(True)**	REVOLUTIONARY WAR	The (Tea) Act made colonial merchants pay taxes on tea.

TEC61067   TEC61067

REVOLUTIONARY WAR	The Sons of _____ caused lots of trouble for tax collectors after the Stamp Act of 1765. **(a) Liberty** (b) Parliament (c) King George	REVOLUTIONARY WAR	**True or False:** The minutemen were afraid to fight and stayed home on April 19, 1775. **(False)**

TEC61067   TEC61067

REVOLUTIONARY WAR	The (Stamp) Act of 1765 said that every important paper had to have a special tax stamp on it to make it legal.	REVOLUTIONARY WAR	The first shot of the Revolutionary War was fired by _____. (a) the British soldiers (b) the colonists **(c) no one knows**

TEC61067   TEC61067

REVOLUTIONARY WAR	**True or False:** The colonists were upset with the king for signing the Tea Act. **(True)**	REVOLUTIONARY WAR	The British went to Concord to find the rebels' hidden (weapons).

TEC61067   TEC61067

©The Mailbox® • *Fascinating Facts: Social Studies* • TEC61067

REVOLUTIONARY WAR

True or False:

The Battle of Bunker Hill was fought on Bunker Hill.

(False)

TEC61067

REVOLUTIONARY WAR

The Americans lost the Battle of Bunker Hill because _____.
(a) they ran out of gunpowder
(b) they were outnumbered
(c) they were afraid of the British

TEC61067

REVOLUTIONARY WAR

Colonel William Prescott told (<u>American Patriots</u>) at the Battle of Bunker Hill, "Don't one of you fire until you see the whites of their eyes."

TEC61067

REVOLUTIONARY WAR

True or False:

The Declaration of Independence said that the colonies would no longer be a part of Britain.

(True)

TEC61067

REVOLUTIONARY WAR

The Declaration of Independence was written by _____.

(a) Abraham Lincoln
(b) Thomas Jefferson
(c) George Washington

TEC61067

REVOLUTIONARY WAR

The Declaration of Independence said that the government should be for the (<u>people</u>).

TEC61067

WESTWARD MOVEMENT

True or False:

Daniel Boone never made it to the great hunting lands of Kentucky.

(False)

TEC61067

WESTWARD MOVEMENT

Daniel Boone claimed almost _____ acres of land.

(a) 100,000
(b) 75,000
(c) 50,000

TEC61067

WESTWARD MOVEMENT

The (<u>Wilderness Road</u>) opened Kentucky to thousands of settlers.

TEC61067

WESTWARD MOVEMENT

True or False:

The United States paid France about $15 million for the Louisiana Territory.

(True)

TEC61067

Game Cards

WESTWARD MOVEMENT

_____ was president of the United States during the Louisiana Purchase.

(a) George Washington
(b) John Adams
(c) Thomas Jefferson

TEC61067

WESTWARD MOVEMENT

True or False:

Sacagawea served as a guide for the Lewis and Clark expedition.

(False)

TEC61067

WESTWARD MOVEMENT

The United States wanted New Orleans because it was a valuable (port).

TEC61067

WESTWARD MOVEMENT

Sacagawea was a _____ Indian.

(a) Shoshone
(b) Navajo
(c) Hidatsa

TEC61067

WESTWARD MOVEMENT

True or False:

The journey by Lewis and Clark into the Louisiana Territory and west took two years.

(True)

TEC61067

WESTWARD MOVEMENT

Sacagawea helped Lewis and Clark gain (horses) from the Shoshones.

TEC61067

WESTWARD MOVEMENT

Meriwether Lewis and William Clark faced _____ on their journey west.

(a) harsh weather
(b) lack of food
(c) both a and b

TEC61067

THE CONSTITUTION

True or False:

The U.S. Constitution remained in a Fort Knox vault during World War II.

(True)

TEC61067

WESTWARD MOVEMENT

Lewis and Clark started their expedition into the Louisiana Territory and west near (St. Louis), Missouri.

TEC61067

THE CONSTITUTION

During the War of 1812, the U.S. Constitution was hidden in a _____.

(a) safe
(b) mill
(c) vault

TEC61067

©The Mailbox® • Fascinating Facts: Social Studies • TEC61067

THE CONSTITUTION — The U.S. Constitution is currently on display in the National (<u>Archives</u>) Building in Washington, DC. TEC61067	**THE CONSTITUTION** — The U.S. Constitution was signed by _____ delegates. (a) eight **(b) 39** (c) 25 TEC61067
THE CONSTITUTION — **True or False:** James Madison was the tenth president of the United States. **(False)** TEC61067	**THE CONSTITUTION** — (<u>William Jackson</u>) witnessed the signing of the U.S. Constitution. TEC61067
THE CONSTITUTION — _____ purchased James Madison's notes from the Constitutional Convention for $30,000. (a) A newspaper (b) The president **(c) Congress** TEC61067	**THE CONSTITUTION** — **True or False:** The Bill of Rights was written by Thomas Jefferson. **(False)** TEC61067
THE CONSTITUTION — James Madison's nickname was the Great (<u>Little</u>) Madison. TEC61067	**THE CONSTITUTION** — The Bill of Rights was added to the U.S. Constitution in _____. **(a) 1791** (b) 1962 (c) 1812 TEC61067
THE CONSTITUTION — **True or False:** The U.S. Constitution was signed on September 17, 1787. **(True)** TEC61067	**THE CONSTITUTION** — The Bill of Rights contains the first (<u>ten</u>) amendments to the U.S. Constitution. TEC61067

Game Cards

U.S. GOVERNMENT	**True or False:** Under the Articles of Confederation, state governments made their own laws. **(True)** TEC61067	U.S. GOVERNMENT	If a president does not support a bill sent to him, he can (veto) it. TEC61067
U.S. GOVERNMENT	The U.S. Constitution established a strong _____ government. (a) state **(b) federal** (c) judicial TEC61067	U.S. GOVERNMENT	**True or False:** Every state has two U.S. senators. **(True)** TEC61067
U.S. GOVERNMENT	Under the Articles of Confederation, the United States had a (weak) central government. TEC61067	U.S. GOVERNMENT	The number of U.S. representatives for a state depends on its _____. (a) size (b) location **(c) population** TEC61067
U.S. GOVERNMENT	**True or False:** The president's term lasts six years. **(False)** TEC61067	U.S. GOVERNMENT	The legislative branch consists of the House of Representatives and the (Senate). TEC61067
U.S. GOVERNMENT	_____ takes over if something happens to the president. **(a) The vice president** (b) The first lady (c) Congress TEC61067	U.S. GOVERNMENT	**True or False:** The judicial court is the highest court in the United States. **(False)** TEC61067

©The Mailbox® • Fascinating Facts: Social Studies • TEC61067

U.S. GOVERNMENT	There are _____ judges on the U.S. Supreme Court. **(a) nine** (b) six (c) three TEC61067	CITIZENSHIP & NATIONAL SYMBOLS	**True or False:** Every person in America can vote. **(False)** TEC61067
U.S. GOVERNMENT	The (U.S. Supreme Court) can rule that a law is unconstitutional. TEC61067	CITIZENSHIP & NATIONAL SYMBOLS	Only about _____ of the people signed up to vote really do vote. **(a) half** (b) one-fourth (c) two-thirds TEC61067
U.S. GOVERNMENT	**True or False:** The legislative branch can impeach a president. **(True)** TEC61067	CITIZENSHIP & NATIONAL SYMBOLS	A U.S. citizen has to be at least (18) years old to vote. TEC61067
U.S. GOVERNMENT	_____ has the power to override a presidential veto. **(a) Congress** (b) The president (c) The Supreme Court TEC61067	CITIZENSHIP & NATIONAL SYMBOLS	**True or False:** The first Pledge of Allegiance was printed in a children's magazine. **(True)** TEC61067
U.S. GOVERNMENT	A system of checks and balances prevents one branch from having too much (power). TEC61067	CITIZENSHIP & NATIONAL SYMBOLS	The first Pledge of Allegiance was written by _____. (a) Christopher Columbus (b) George Washington **(c) Francis Bellamy**

Game Cards

<table>
<tr>
<td>CITIZENSHIP & NATIONAL SYMBOLS</td>
<td>In 1892, when the Pledge of Allegiance was written, schoolchildren were asked to say the pledge and fly the (<u>flag</u>).

TEC61067</td>
<td>CITIZENSHIP & NATIONAL SYMBOLS</td>
<td>"The Star-Spangled Banner" is about the United States's _____.

(a) seal
(b) geography
(c) flag

TEC61067</td>
</tr>
<tr>
<td>CITIZENSHIP & NATIONAL SYMBOLS</td>
<td>**True or False:**

A 17-year-old designed the 50-star U.S. flag in 1958.

(True)

TEC61067</td>
<td>CITIZENSHIP & NATIONAL SYMBOLS</td>
<td>("The Star-Spangled Banner") was made our national anthem in 1931.

TEC61067</td>
</tr>
<tr>
<td>CITIZENSHIP & NATIONAL SYMBOLS</td>
<td>The current U.S. flag has ____ stripes.

(a) 12
(b) 13
(c) 15

TEC61067</td>
<td>CITIZENSHIP & NATIONAL SYMBOLS</td>
<td>**True or False:**

Benjamin Franklin wanted the turkey to be the national symbol of the United States.

(True)

TEC61067</td>
</tr>
<tr>
<td>CITIZENSHIP & NATIONAL SYMBOLS</td>
<td>A star is added every time a (<u>state</u>) joins the Union.

TEC61067</td>
<td>CITIZENSHIP & NATIONAL SYMBOLS</td>
<td>The bald eagle is found in _____.

(a) Europe
(b) Great Britain
(c) North America

TEC61067</td>
</tr>
<tr>
<td>CITIZENSHIP & NATIONAL SYMBOLS</td>
<td>**True or False:**

Francis Scott Key wrote the music to "The Star-Spangled Banner."

(False)

TEC61067</td>
<td>CITIZENSHIP & NATIONAL SYMBOLS</td>
<td>In 1782, Congress made the (<u>bald eagle</u>) the national symbol.

TEC61067</td>
</tr>
</table>

©The Mailbox® • Fascinating Facts: Social Studies • TEC61067

CITIZENSHIP & NATIONAL SYMBOLS

True or False:

The Capitol is the home of the president of the United States.

(False)

TEC61067

CITIZENSHIP & NATIONAL SYMBOLS

A _____ was built under the Capitol Rotunda.

(a) storeroom

(b) burial place for George Washington

(c) meeting room for the U.S. Senate

TEC61067

CITIZENSHIP & NATIONAL SYMBOLS

A huge (dome) covers the Capitol Rotunda.

TEC61067

CITIZENSHIP & NATIONAL SYMBOLS

True or False:

The Washington Monument was started while George Washington was alive.

(False)

TEC61067

CITIZENSHIP & NATIONAL SYMBOLS

The Washington Monument is the tallest stone structure in _____.

(a) Washington, DC

(b) the nation

(c) the world

TEC61067

CITIZENSHIP & NATIONAL SYMBOLS

(The Washington Monument) is a four-sided figure called an obelisk.

TEC61067

CITIZENSHIP & NATIONAL SYMBOLS

True or False:

The Statue of Liberty was the first electric lighthouse.

(True)

TEC61067

CITIZENSHIP & NATIONAL SYMBOLS

_____ gave the Statue of Liberty to the United States.

(a) Britain

(b) China

(c) France

TEC61067

CITIZENSHIP & NATIONAL SYMBOLS

The Statue of Liberty is now cared for by the (National Park Service).

TEC61067

CITIZENSHIP & NATIONAL SYMBOLS

True or False:

The Liberty Bell has only cracked once.

(False)

TEC61067

Game Cards

<table>
<tr>
<td>CITIZENSHIP & NATIONAL SYMBOLS</td>
<td>The Liberty Bell was rung to _____.

(a) call people together for special announcements
(b) chime the hour
(c) make people complain about the noise

TEC61067</td>
<td>HISTORIC FIGURES</td>
<td>**True or False:**

Thomas Jefferson's most famous piece of writing is the Declaration of Independence.

(True)

TEC61067</td>
</tr>
<tr>
<td>CITIZENSHIP & NATIONAL SYMBOLS</td>
<td>People go to the city of (<u>Philadelphia</u>) to see the Liberty Bell.

TEC61067</td>
<td>HISTORIC FIGURES</td>
<td>Thomas Jefferson was a skilled _____.

(a) athlete
(b) inventor
(c) dancer

TEC61067</td>
</tr>
<tr>
<td>HISTORIC FIGURES</td>
<td>**True or False:**

No one voted against George Washington in the election that made him president of the United States.

(True)

TEC61067</td>
<td>HISTORIC FIGURES</td>
<td>Thomas Jefferson sold his personal (<u>library</u>) to the Library of Congress.

TEC61067</td>
</tr>
<tr>
<td>HISTORIC FIGURES</td>
<td>George Washington is known as the "Father of His _____."

(a) Frontier
(b) Country
(c) Army

TEC61067</td>
<td>HISTORIC FIGURES</td>
<td>**True or False:**

Ben Franklin was an inventor and a teacher.

(False)

TEC61067</td>
</tr>
<tr>
<td>HISTORIC FIGURES</td>
<td>George Washington led the army of colonists during the Revolutionary War to win independence from (<u>Great Britain</u>).

TEC61067</td>
<td>HISTORIC FIGURES</td>
<td>Ben Franklin created _____.

(a) a kite
(b) a cooking stove
(c) bifocals

TEC61067</td>
</tr>
</table>

©The Mailbox® • Fascinating Facts: Social Studies • TEC61067

HISTORIC FIGURES — Ben Franklin never made (money) from any of his inventions. TEC61067	**HISTORIC FIGURES** — Abigail Adams urged her husband to "remember the _____." (a) children (b) soldiers **(c) ladies** TEC61067
HISTORIC FIGURES — **True or False:** Paul Revere was arrested for helping the patriots. **(False)** TEC61067	**HISTORIC FIGURES** — Abigail Adams was the wife of one president and the (mother) of another. TEC61067
HISTORIC FIGURES — One way Paul Revere helped the patriot cause was by _____. (a) giving speeches (b) giving food **(c) printing paper money** TEC61067	**HISTORIC FIGURES** — **True or False:** Dolley Madison was a famous hostess. **(True)** TEC61067
HISTORIC FIGURES — Paul Revere risked his life so America could be free from (British) rule. TEC61067	**HISTORIC FIGURES** — Dolley Madison saved _____ when the British army attacked the White House. **(a) a painting** (b) gold (c) the U.S. Constitution TEC61067
HISTORIC FIGURES — **True or False:** Abigail Adams is famous for writing poems to her husband. **(False)** TEC61067	**HISTORIC FIGURES** — Dolley Madison's husband James was the (fourth) president. TEC61067

Game Cards

HISTORIC FIGURES	**True or False:** Phillis Wheatley wrote books for children. **(False)** TEC61067	**HISTORIC FIGURES**	Sojourner Truth raised money for black troops during the (Civil) War. TEC61067
HISTORIC FIGURES	Phillis Wheatley was invited to meet General _____ after writing a poem to honor him. **(a) Washington** (b) Adams (c) Boston TEC61067	**HISTORIC FIGURES**	**True or False:** Harriet Tubman never received any honors for her role with the Underground Railroad. **(False)** TEC61067
HISTORIC FIGURES	Phillis Wheatley traveled to (England), where her poetry book was published. TEC61067	**HISTORIC FIGURES**	Harriet Tubman helped the _____ army during the Civil War. (a) Confederate (b) Canadian **(c) Union** TEC61067
HISTORIC FIGURES	**True or False:** Sojourner Truth could not read or write. **(True)** TEC61067	**HISTORIC FIGURES**	Harriet Tubman escaped (slavery) and found freedom via the Underground Railroad. TEC61067
HISTORIC FIGURES	Sojourner Truth helped _____. (a) write speeches for the president **(b) escaped slaves find jobs** (c) slaves on the Underground Railroad TEC61067	**HISTORIC FIGURES**	**True or False:** Frederick Douglass was an escaped slave. **(True)** TEC61067

©The Mailbox® • Fascinating Facts: Social Studies • TEC61067

HISTORIC FIGURES

Frederick Douglass worked with President _____ to end slavery.

(a) Lincoln
(b) Washington
(c) Adams

TEC61067

U.S. REGIONS

True or False:

A megalopolis is a group of cities that have expanded and grown together.

(True)

TEC61067

HISTORIC FIGURES

Frederick Douglass was known for his speeches against (slavery).

TEC61067

U.S. REGIONS

The largest megalopolis in the United States is found in the _____ region.

(a) northeastern
(b) southeastern
(c) midwestern

TEC61067

HISTORIC FIGURES

True or False:

George Washington Carver is famous for his work with peanuts.

(True)

TEC61067

U.S. REGIONS

The deep (harbors) in the Northeast make the area good for shipping.

TEC61067

HISTORIC FIGURES

George Washington Carver was called the Plant _____.

(a) Farmer
(b) Doctor
(c) Nurse

TEC61067

U.S. REGIONS

True or False:

Many NASCAR races are held in the southeastern states.

(True)

TEC61067

HISTORIC FIGURES

George Washington Carver made more than 300 products from (peanuts).

TEC61067

U.S. REGIONS

Stock car racing began in the _____ United States.

(a) northeastern
(b) southeastern
(c) midwestern

TEC61067

Game Cards

<table>
<tr>
<td>**U.S. REGIONS**

When visitors come to the southeastern United States to enjoy the mountains, beaches, theme parks, and races, they help support the region's (tourism) industry.

TEC61067</td>
<td>**U.S. REGIONS**

Rich soil makes the Midwest a perfect place for _____.

(a) tourism
(b) farms
(c) government

TEC61067</td>
</tr>
<tr>
<td>**U.S. REGIONS**

True or False:

Arizona, New Mexico, Texas, and Oklahoma are states in the Southwest.

(True)

TEC61067</td>
<td>**U.S. REGIONS**

The United States region known for its flatland is the (Midwest).

TEC61067</td>
</tr>
<tr>
<td>**U.S. REGIONS**

The southwestern states are known for their record-breaking _____.

(a) temperatures
(b) age of trees
(c) snowfalls

TEC61067</td>
<td>**U.S. REGIONS**

True or False:

Forests are an important resource in the western United States.

(True)

TEC61067</td>
</tr>
<tr>
<td>**U.S. REGIONS**

Some of the hottest temperatures in the United States are in the (Southwestern) region.

TEC61067</td>
<td>**U.S. REGIONS**

Oregon, Washington, and ____ are top lumber-producing states.

(a) California
(b) Arizona
(c) Nevada

TEC61067</td>
</tr>
<tr>
<td>**U.S. REGIONS**

True or False:

The midwestern region of the United States is a mountainous area.

(False)

TEC61067</td>
<td>**U.S. REGIONS**

The state of (California) has some of the earth's largest and oldest trees.

TEC61067</td>
</tr>
</table>

©The Mailbox® • Fascinating Facts: Social Studies • TEC61067

Answer Keys

Page 5
1. Europeans wanted the gold and spices that were there.
2. about ten weeks
3. four
4. People on two continents were exposed to new plants, animals, and diseases.

Page 6
1. GENOA, ITALY
2. OTTOMAN EMPIRE
3. FERDINAND, ISABELLA
4. CIRCUMFERENCE
5. CARAVELS
6. MUTINY
7. TAINO

Page 7
1. Florida
2. Columbus
3. the island of Puerto Rico
4. north of Cuba
5. arrow

Page 8

v	o	y	a	g	e				
		P	u	e	r	t	o		
		c	l	a	i	m	e	d	
		F	o	u	n	t	a	i	n
H	i	s	p	a	n	i	o	l	a
a	t	t	a	c	k	e	d		
F	e	r	d	i	n	a	n	d	
c	o	l	o	n	i	z	e		
		S	p	a	i	n			
			m	i	n	e			

GULF STREAM.

Page 9
1. 1,300
2. north
3. New Mexico
4. gold
5. Southwest

Page 10
1. The Spanish had heard tales of golden cities, so they wanted to explore the American Southwest.
2. Coronado was determined to find the Seven Cities of Cibola because he believed they held great wealth.
3. A priest was chosen to go on the journey since he claimed to have seen one of the golden cities.
4. When they reached the city and found no gold, the men became discouraged.
5. Coronado and his men became excited when they heard about another golden city in the east.
6. Because they wanted to find the gold, the men marched all the way to Kansas.
7. They were disappointed again since the stories weren't true.
8. Because Coronado found no gold or riches, his trip was seen as a failure.

> —— = green
> —— = yellow

Page 11
1. La Salle explored the ~~Ohio~~ Mississippi River.
2. La Salle hoped to gain more wealth by continuing to trade ~~land~~ furs.
3. His journey down the Mississippi River ended at the Gulf of ~~California~~ Mexico.
4. He claimed the lands around the river and its tributaries for ~~Spain~~ France.

Page 12
1. true
2. true
3. false
4. false
5. false
6. true
7. true
8. false
9. false
10. false

Page 13
1. c
2. a
3. a
4. b

Page 14
Sentences will vary. Accept reasonable answers.
1. ST. LAWRENCE
2. QUEBEC
3. LAKE CHAMPLAIN
4. LAKE ONTARIO
5. PANAMA CANAL

Page 15
1. true
2. false
3. false
4. true
5. false

Page 16
1. compass
2. astrolabe
3. cross-staff
4. quadrant
5. sundial
6. nocturnal
7. sandglass
8. pincer

Page 17
1. the Jamestown colony did well.
2. to find gold and start a new colony
3. or go without food.
4. he was wounded.
5. were afraid of Smith.

Page 18
1. F
2. C
3. A
4. B
5. E
6. D

Page 19
1. soldiers
2. important paper
3. representation
4. Sons of Liberty
5. 1766

Page 20

To Our American Colonists:
    We need money to pay the British ___**soldiers**___ in America. These soldiers protect you. So we have passed a new law. We call it the ___**Stamp Act**___ _____. You will need a special ___**stamp**___ for each important ___**paper**___. You will have to pay for each stamp.

                    Sincerely,
                    King George and the
                    British ___**Parliament**___

To King George and the British Parliament:
    We are ___**angry**___! Why should we pay taxes? ___**Colonists**___ are not allowed to serve in Parliament. Making us pay ___**taxes**___ without a say is not right! The Sons of Liberty will scare your tax ___**collectors**___, and they will not be able to sell the stamps.

                    Sincerely,
                    The ___**American**___ Colonists

Page 21
1. true
2. false
3. true
4. false
5. false

Page 22
1. "What do you mean the king says I still have to pay taxes on tea sold by colonial merchants?"
2. "Send those ships back to England!"
3. "You must obey the king's orders. You must obey the Tea Act!"
4. "Psst. The king has gone too far this time!" "Boston Harbor will be a teapot tonight!"
5. December 16, 1773—The Boston Tea Party
6. "I'll show the colonists who's boss! Now they'll have even more rules to follow."

Page 23
1. The ~~minutemen~~ *redcoats* wanted to capture the colonists' weapons.
2. Before arriving in Lexington, the British marched all ~~day~~ *night*.
3. The British marched on to ~~Boston~~ *Concord* after the Battle of Lexington.
4. The ~~British~~ *colonists* hid along the road, waiting to attack.
5. It was ~~hard~~ *easy* to see the British coming in their redcoats.
6. The Battles of Lexington and Concord were the ~~end~~ *beginning* of the Revolutionary War.

Page 24

Crossword:
1 down: Revolutionary
2 down: Lexington
3 across: Paul Revere
4 across: minutemen
5 across: Boston
6 down: Concord
7 across: Hancock
8 across: redcoats
(1 across: Rebels)

Page 25
1. b
2. c
3. b
4. c

Page 26
1. I
2. E
3. R
4. D
5. L
6. B
7. S
8. H
9. L
10. E

<u>BREED'S HILL</u>

Page 27
1. peace
2. army
3. world
4. rights
5. nation

Page 28
1. b
2. g
3. c
4. f
5. a
6. d
7. e

Page 29
1. outdoors
2. Wilderness Road
3. 100,000
4. Boonesborough
5. Missouri

Page 30
1. pioneer
2. Pennsylvania
3. Wilderness
4. Cumberland
5. settle
6. fort
7. Boonesborough
8. claimed

Page 31
1. goods
2. France
3. port
4. Louisiana Purchase
5. $15 million

Page 32

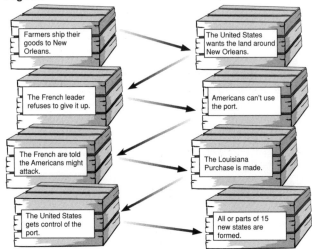

Farmers ship their goods to New Orleans.
The French leader refuses to give it up.
The French are told the Americans might attack.
The United States gets control of the port.
The United States wants the land around New Orleans.
Americans can't use the port.
The Louisiana Purchase is made.
All or parts of 15 new states are formed.

122

Page 33
1. c
2. c
3. b
4. a
5. c

Page 34
1. red
2. red
3. red
4. brown
5. red
6. brown
7. red
8. brown
9. brown
10. red
11. brown
12. red

Page 35
1. false
2. true
3. false
4. false
5. true
6. true

Page 36
1. brown
2. orange
3. orange
4. brown
5. orange
6. orange
7. brown
8. brown

Page 37
1. c
2. d
3. e
4. f
5. a
6. b

Page 38

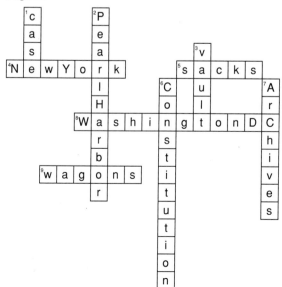

Page 39
1. journals
2. shortest
3. Father
4. Philadelphia
5. elected
6. Montpelier

Page 40
1. Virginia
2. sick
3. Montpelier
4. Jefferson
5. notes
6. secret
7. Rights
8. Dolley
9. fourth
10. War

Page 41
1. b
2. c
3. b
4. b

Page 42
1. BENJAMIN FRANKLIN
2. JONATHAN DAYTON
3. GEORGE WASHINGTON
4. RHODE ISLAND
5. INDEPENDENCE HALL
6. MADISON and WASHINGTON
7. DECLARATION OF INDEPENDENCE

Page 43
1. false
2. true
3. false
4. false
5. true
6. true

Page 44
A. 4
B. 3
C. 1
D. 6
E. 2
F. 10
G. 5
H. 1
I. 1

Page 45
1. b
2. a
3. b
4. c

Page 46
Federal Government
makes treaties
sets up post offices

Both Governments
make and enforce laws
build roads

State Government
conducts elections
issues driver's licenses

Page 47
1. false
2. false
3. true
4. false
5. true
6. true

Page 48
1. 1951
2. 20
3. $400,000
4. 15
5. eight
6. 46
7. three
8. 1841

CONGRESS

Page 49
1. The legislative branch has ~~three~~ two parts.
2. Every senator serves a ~~two~~ six-year term.
3. A state's number of members in the House of Representatives is based on the state's number of ~~cities~~ people.
4. A member of Congress is elected by people who live in ~~another~~ her state.
5. Senators have a ~~shorter~~ longer term in office than representatives.

Page 50
1. voters
2. limit
3. Compromise
4. Capitol Hill
5. Freedom
6. make laws

L	A	C	S	W	D	R	S	B	F	Q	G
D	K	F	R	Y	J	G	V	W	R	M	V
K	L	I	M	I	T	J	O	I	A	P	F
H	B	E	T	U	Z	A	T	K	E	J	Y
F	N	V	U	N	K	M	E	S	I	N	K
O	R	Y	C	O	C	L	R	C	A	E	D
P	G	E	Q	Z	A	H	S	V	L	I	V
A	X	L	E	W	X	Q	F	I	T	J	X
H	Q	T	S	D	G	W	T	O	M	D	M
L	L	I	H	L	O	T	I	P	A	C	W
M	H	E	C	B	L	M	P	S	N	Z	B
U	W	C	O	M	P	R	O	M	I	S	E

Page 51
1. rules
2. judicial
3. Supreme
4. nine
5. fairly, Constitution

Page 52
1. D
2. F
3. C
4. I
5. J
6. A
7. G
8. B
9. E
10. H

Page 53
1. sometimes
2. always
3. sometimes
4. never
5. always
6. sometimes

Page 54
Executive Branch: writes the nation's budget, appoints Supreme Court justices
Legislative Branch: can impeach a president or vice president, must approve all Supreme Court appointments
Judicial Branch: can rule that a decision made by the president is unconstitutional, decides the meaning of laws

Page 55
1. To vote in the United States, one must be at least ~~21~~ 18 years old.
2. Only U.S. ~~tourists~~ citizens can vote in a U.S. election.
3. Americans have been voting since the founding of ~~Canada~~ the United States.
4. People vote on many different ~~votes~~ issues.
5. The number of votes is ~~never~~ sometimes close.

Page 56

1. 1 9 0 0 s
2. P u n c h
3. f i r s t
4. u n f a i r
5. r a c e s
6. p a p e r
7. C o l l e g e
8. v o t e

suffrage

124

Page 57

Answers will vary but should contain the following:

1. The Pledge of Allegiance was written to honor the 400th anniversary of Christopher Columbus's first trip to the Americas.
2. The pledge was printed in *The Youth's Companion* and on leaflets sent throughout the country.
3. More than 12 million schoolchildren recited the pledge on October 12, 1892.
4. In 1923 and 1924, the words *my flag* were changed to *the Flag of the United States of America*. In 1954, the words *under God* were added.

Page 58

1. C
2. F
3. B
4. E
5. A
6. D

Page 59

5 Robert's teacher changed his grade.
2 Robert spent 12½ hours making his flag.
3 Robert's teacher gave him a B–.
1 Robert Heft designed a new flag.
4 Robert's congressman got Congress to approve his new design.

Page 60

Respect for the Flag: 3, 4, 6, 7, 10
When to Display the Flag: 1, 2, 5, 8, 9

Page 61

1. flag
2. Great Britain
3. Fort McHenry
4. poem
5. anthem

Page 62

1. blue
2. red
3. red
4. blue
5. blue
6. red
7. red
8. blue
9. red
10. blue

Page 63

Answers may vary.

1. Benjamin Franklin wanted the ~~eagle~~ turkey to be our national symbol.
2. People thought the bald eagle was a ~~weak~~ strong bird.
3. In 1782, ~~Franklin~~ Congress made the bald eagle a national symbol.
4. The bald eagle's picture can be found on money and state ~~buttons~~ seals.
5. The bald eagle is a ~~weak~~ powerful symbol.

Page 64

Bald Eagle: A, D, H, I, J
Both: C, F
North American Turkey: B, E, G, K, L

Page 65

1. false
2. true
3. true
4. false
5. false
6. false

Page 66

1. SAMUEL ADAMS
2. JAMES GARFIELD
3. SAM HOUSTON
4. WILL ROGERS
5. ETHAN ALLEN
6. ROBERT FULTON

Page 67

1. because it would be too expensive.
2. money to build the monument.
3. memorial stones.
4. an obelisk.
5. in 1884.

Page 68

1. FATHER OF THE COUNTRY
2. FUNDS
3. ROBERT MILLS
4. GRANITE
5. FIFTEEN
6. NINETY
7. HOLLOW
8. EIGHT HUNDRED NINETY-SIX

Page 69
1. French
2. *Liberty Enlightening the World*
3. crown
4. lighthouse
5. National Park Service
6. Millions
7. 151, 225
8. 2.4

Page 70
1. E
2. M
3. A
4. L
5. Z
6. R
7. U
8. S

<u>EMMA LAZARUS</u>

Page 71
1. The bell was made to observe the 50th anniversary of the Pennsylvania colony.
2. It was rung to call people to a public reading of the Declaration of Independence.
3. It was hidden to keep it from being made into a cannon.
4. Answers may vary but should mention that people who were against slavery renamed it the Liberty Bell.
5. People stopped ringing the bell because it cracked again.
6. Answers may vary.

Page 72

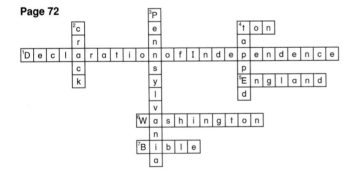

Page 73
1. true
2. false
3. false
4. true
5. true

Page 74
1732: George Washington was born in Virginia in 1732.

1749: Washington was 17 when he was hired to survey land in Virginia.

1754: Five years after being hired as a land surveyor, he was a colonel in the French and Indian War.

1755–58: One year after being in the French and Indian War, he served three years as colonel of Virginia's frontier troops.

1775: Washington was 43 years old when he became commander in chief of the Continental Army.

1781: Six years after he became commander in chief, he won the battle that ended the Revolutionary War.

1787: He became president of the Constitutional Convention 55 years after he was born.

1789: At age 57, George Washington became the first president of the United States.

Page 75
Sentences will vary but should contain the following:
1. The library was created for members of Congress.
2. The books were burned during the War of 1812.
3. Jefferson offered his collection of books to the library.
4. Today, the library can be used by anyone; it is the largest library in the world.

Page 76
Architect: 3, 4, 12
Musician: 1, 7, 8
Scientist: 2, 6, 9
Inventor: 5, 10, 11

Page 77
1. b
2. c
3. a
4. a
5. c

Page 78
1. A PENNY SAVED IS A PENNY EARNED.
2. BETTER SLIP WITH FOOT THAN TONGUE.
3. GREAT TALKERS, LITTLE DOERS.
4. 'TIS EASY TO SEE, HARD TO FORESEE.

Page 79
1. arrested
2. lanterns
3. Lexington
4. patriots
5. horse

Page 80

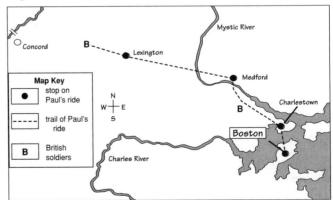

Page 81
1. wife
2. letters
3. colonies
4. British
5. women

Page 82
1. WEYMOUTH
2. HEALTH
3. LIBRARY
4. JOHN ADAMS
5. FIVE
6. SIXTH
7. CONGRESS
8. SCHOOLING
9. REVOLUTIONARY
10. SLAVERY

Page 83
1. Dolley was married to the ~~14th~~ fourth president.
2. Dolley's guests always felt ~~worried~~ welcome.
3. The British ~~painted~~ burned the White House during the War of 1812.
4. The first lady ~~donated~~ saved a famous portrait of George Washington.

Page 84
1. purple
2. green
3. green
4. purple
5. purple
6. green
7. green
8. purple

Page 85
1. Phillis was brought to Boston to be sold as a slave.
2. The Wheatleys taught her to read and write.
3. Phillis's first poem was published in a newspaper.
4. She had written a poem in his honor.

Page 86
1. KIDNAPPED, BOSTON, *PHILLIS*
2. LETTERS, ELEGIES, DIED, LEADERS
3. ENGLAND, FRANKLIN, KING GEORGE, ILL
4. FREEDOM, MARRIED, SHORT

Page 87
1. Isabella Baumfree
2. slavery
3. voice, words
4. Dutch, English
5. money

Page 88
1. B, a person who helps others gain <u>equal</u> rights
2. H, the practice of <u>owning</u> people and forcing them to work
3. F, a place to <u>buy</u> and sell slaves
4. A, a person who wanted to <u>end</u> slavery
5. C, a person who tries to <u>escape</u>
6. E, Sojourner Truth's birth <u>name</u>
7. G, a conflict between citizens of the <u>same</u> country
8. D, a person forced to <u>work</u> as the property of another

Page 89
1. slave
2. secret paths
3. slavery
4. Union army
5. honored

Page 90
1. mother
2. rock
3. Canada
4. family
5. reward
6. spy

Page 91
1. true
2. false
3. false
4. true
5. false
6. true
7. true
8. false

Page 92
1. FREEDOM
2. MINORITIES
3. FEBRUARY
4. AUTOBIOGRAPHY
5. LINCOLN
6. SLAVE
7. NEWSPAPER
8. PRESIDENT

Page 93
1. strong
2. garden
3. nurse
4. agriculture
5. rotate
6. research

Page 94
1. He was a sickly child and not very strong.
2. He could nurse sick plants back to health.
3. Growing only cotton depleted, or wore out, the soil.
4. George wanted to help farmers.
5. He did a lot of research on peanuts.
6. George also created products from sweet potatoes and pecans.

Page 95
1. The area from Boston to Washington, DC, is a ~~metropolis~~ megalopolis.
2. People use more ~~private~~ public transportation in a large city.
3. ~~Few~~ Many people live in the northeastern megalopolis.
4. The ~~midwestern~~ northeastern megalopolis stretches for about 600 miles.
5. The ~~shallow~~ deep ports make the Northeast a good place for worldwide trade.

Page 96
Northeastern Megalopolis Cities: Baltimore; New York City; Boston; Washington, DC; Philadelphia

Northeastern Industries: finance, communications, tourism, medical research, factories

Northeastern Public Transportation: boats, trolleys, taxis, buses, subways, airplanes

Page 97
1. c
2. c
3. b
4. c

Page 98
1. STONE MOUNTAIN
2. WILLIAMSBURG
3. MAMMOTH CAVE
4. FORT MCHENRY
5. U.S. SPACE and ROCKET CENTER
6. CHARLOTTE
7. FLORIDA KEYS
8. HOT SPRINGS NATIONAL PARK

Page 99
1. hottest
2. climates
3. cooler
4. Havasu City
5. difference

Page 100
1. Lake Havasu City
2. New Mexico
3. Tahlequah
4. Petrified Forest National Park
5. San Antonio, Texas
6. Carlsbad Caverns National Park
7. Oklahoma City
8. Houston, Texas

Page 101
1. growing
2. people, animals
3. cereal
4. Wisconsin
5. Answers will vary but should include that much of the food for the nation is produced in this region.

Page 102
1. Deere
2. Cows
3. hogs
4. wheat
5. soybeans
6. people
7. McCormick
8. cities
9. Ohio
10. Irrigation

Thanks, Midwest!

Page 103
1. The region makes money from timber production.
2. An effect of cutting old trees might be that endangered species could die out.
3. Trees help preserve water by soaking up rain and preventing runoff.
4. Sequoia trees can grow up to 300 feet tall and 100 feet around.

Page 104
Facts: 1, 3, 4, 6, 7, 10
Opinions: 2, 5, 8, 9